PyQt6 101

A Beginner's guide to PyQt6

Edward Chang

PyQt6 101: A Beginner's guide to PyQt6

Edward Chang

ISBN: 9798328983730

Table of Contents

This page inten-
tionally left blank

List of Figures

Preface to the 2nd Edition

Thanks to the support of my readers, I'm back with the 2nd edition of this book.

This second edition attempts to bring the original up to date by thorough revision, and, addition of a new chapter that reviews Object-oriented Programming(OOP). Also, running some of the apps in the book has been problematic for some users because of the app dependencies. A Dockerfile that runs all the apps in this book and installs all the required dependencies has been provided.

1. Book source code

Source code for the book can be found at:

https://gitlab.com/wohlstetter/pyqt6-101-2ndedition

This page inten-
tionally left blank

Preface to the 1st Edition

I could bore you with a lot of theory about Python, the history of user interface (U.I.) design and so on. But, I trust that you'll be able to research all the dreary stuff when(if ever!) you need it. Instead, like Neo in the Matrix, we'll skip all the boring stuff and get right to the meat and potatoes of the subject.

The only assumptions I make are:

1. That you're acquainted with the basics of Python. You can always refer to:
   https://docs.python.org/3/tutorial/
   if you're a bit rusty.
2. Some experience using the command line interface (CLI) on your operating system.
3. Know how to install python modules.
4. Basic knowledge of the HTTP protocol.
5. Basic knowledge of MySQL databases. A brief overview can be found at:
   https://www.tutorialspoint.com/sql/sql-overview.htm
   A beautifully designed e-book with more details can be found at:
   https://goalkicker.com/SQLBook/

It also helps to have experience with a "visual" programming language like Visual Basic, Delphi or mobile phone programming. But, it's not necessary.

1. Conventions used

There are a number of text conventions used throughout this book.

Italics: Used for a new term, an important word, or words, function names, variable names, command-line input and code in text. Here is an example:
Change the button from its default name *pushButton* to *btnBrowse*.

When we wish to draw your attention to a particular part of code or output, the relevant lines or items are set in bold: **Review the last minute of the video to see this!**

 Tip
Tips and tricks appear like this.

Important

Warnings or important notes appear like this.

Note

Notes appear like this.

2. Book source code

Source code for the book can be found at:

https://gitlab.com/wohlstetter/pyqt6-101

3. Images

Some images had to be shrank so they could be displayed in the document. The most important of these can be found in the *images* folder of the source code.

As always, happy coding!

Chapter 1. Object-oriented Programming Refresher

This chapter is mainly intended for beginner Python coders. Experienced Python coders may skip it.

I will not exhaustively cover Object-oriented Programming(OOP). I'll only go over the ideas you need to understand the scripts in this book.

If you want to follow along, you can create a new text file and paste in the following code. Else, this and all other code will be found in the source code that came with your book. The code for each chapter is in a folder named after that chapter.

1.1. Why OOP?

Before OOP, there was procedural programming that divided a program into functions and data that these functions manipulated. A program was like a recipe that sequentially manipulated data to produce the result we wanted.

But as programs grew larger, the overlap between functions and their data often caused unforeseen problems. OOP broke down unwieldy programs into smaller units of related variables and functions called **objects**. We call these variables **attributes** and the functions that manipulate them are called **methods**.

1.2. Classes

A **class** is a representation of an object. It is the blueprint from which individual objects are created.

A simple example of a class can be found in *basicexample.py* in the folder for this chapter.

```
1 class exampleClass:
2     """ A simple example of a class. """
3     i = 5000
```

To create an instance of a class, you use function notation. The following creates an instance of *exampleClass* and returns an object that we assign to a variable named *y*.

```
y = exampleClass()
```

Our object has two attributes: an integer and a docstring which we can access as shown below.

```
>>> y = exampleClass()
>>>
>>> y.i
5000
>>>
>>> y.__doc__
' A simple example of a class. '
>>>
```

1.2.1. Class methods

Methods are functions within a class that are designed to perform a particular task. Python distinguishes between user-defined methods written by a programmer and special methods that are part of the language.

These **magic** methods have a double underscore(**dunder**) on either side of their name for example: *__init__()* .

1.2.2. Object initialisation

Instantiation i.e. calling a class object gives us an empty object. Setting the initial state of objects in Java and C++ is done using a constructor method. The Python equivalent of this is the *__new__()* method.

To see a demonstration of this, open the file called *classes101.py* in a terminal. One way to do this is by typing the following:

```
python3 -i classes101.py
```

The code of class *classDemo* is shown below.

```
1 class classDemo:
```

```
 2      def __new__(cls, *args, **kwargs):
 3          print ('__new__ is the constructor for a
class')
 4          return object.__new__(cls)
 5
 6      def __init__(self, args):
 7          print('__init__ is the initialiser for a
class')
 8
 9      def __del__(self):
10          print('__del__ is the finaliser for a
class')
11
12      def greeting(self):
13          print('__new__ or __init__? Now you know
what get\'s called first :)')
```

When we create an object called *x* as shown, we get the following:

```
>>> x = classDemo('')
__new__ is the constructor for a class
__init__ is the initialiser for a class
```

__new__() is rarely overridden[1] in Python, so we don't need to worry about it at this stage. We'll do all our work in the *__init__*() method, which, as its name suggests, initialises objects. By the time this method is called, the object has already been created. The last line of *__new__*() creates this object which is passed to *__init__*() as its *self* parameter.

The complement of the initialiser method is the finaliser method *__del__*(). This method is called prior to the resources for the object being deallocated. You can see this method being invoked when you close your REPL session, or, if you create an object with the same name more than once.

```
>>> y = classDemo('')
__new__ is the constructor for a class
```

----

[1]Please note this word! The concept of overriding will be explained soon.

```
__init__  is the initialiser for a class
>>>
>>> y = classDemo('')
__new__  is the constructor for a class
__init__  is the initialiser for a class
__del__  is the finaliser for a class
```

1.2.3. What is the nature of *self*?

The *self* variable represents the instance of the object itself. According to the official Python documentation, the name *self* has no special meaning in Python. It's used by convention among programmers to make our code more readable.

As illustrated by the following code, you can use whatever name you like instead of *self*, as long as you use it consistently. Python will use whatever variable name you pass as the first parameter to __init__() as a substitute for *self*.

```
class bananaClassDemo:
    def __init__(banana, name):
        banana._name = name

    def __del__(banana):
        print('This message is from the finaliser method
 of bananaClassDemo')

    def greeting(banana):
        print('Hello', banana._name)
```

Whatever variable name *x* you choose to use to represent your object instance, attributes "attached" to this name persist throughout the object's lifetime. Otherwise if you don't use this name, then the attribute values are forgotten once __init__() goes out of scope. Class *warthogClassDemo* illustrates this:

```
class warthogClassDemo:
    def __init__(self, name):
        _name = name
        print('The value of _name inside the initialiser
 is', _name)
```

```
def __del__(self):
    print('This message is from the finaliser method
of warthogClassDemo')


def greeting(self):
    """ This is here just to remind you that methods
can also have docstrings :) """
    try:
        print('Hello', _name)
    except NameError:
        print('Few creatures are as forgetful as a
warthog. I\'ve already forgotten your name!')
```

When ran I got:

```
>>> y = warthogClassDemo('Joe')
The value of _name inside the initialiser is Joe
>>>
>>> y.greeting()
Few creatures are as forgetful as a warthog. I've
 already forgotten your name!
```

1.3. Inheritance

Inheritance allows new child classes to be created that inherit attributes and methods from their parent classes. The parent class is sometimes referred to as the base class. Inheritance captures meaning in a classification hierarchy, arranging concepts from generalized to specialized.

A little bird tells me that you've been studying too much and that it's time for a break. Let me tell you a story.

1.3.1. Story time

Somewhere in Hungary during the 5th century, a village was ravaged by a plague. Almost everyone was killed except a young man named Alexander Corvinus. Instead of succumbing to the plague like everyone else, his blood bonded and adapted to the plague virus, making him immortal. The Corvinus Strain mutated in him and was passed in its active form to his two sons Marcus and William. Alexander's third son carried the passive form.

Unlike his two brothers, he was born mortal and died, but not before passing the strain to his progeny. As adults William and Marcus were bitten by a wolf and a bat respectively. They both bonded with and adapted to the mixture of virus and animal DNA, from the animals that had bitten them. Two immortal subspecies were spawned: Werewolves(later to give way to Lycans) and Vampires.

In modern times, the family name "Corvinus" survives as "Corvin". The progeny of Alexander's third son carried less of the dormant strain with each successive generation. The family line of Michael Corvin can trace it origins back to Alexander Corvinus via this third son. Michael Corvin's grandparents migrated to America from Hungary in the 1940s. Michael was born there in 1975 and he moved to Hungary in 2003 as a trauma surgeon intern.

Through a convoluted series of events, Michael was bitten first by a Lycan, then by a Vampire. He became the first Lycan-Vampire hybrid. He has all the strengths of both subspecies, but none of their weaknesses.

1.3.2. Back to class

I will use *underworldclass.py* to illustrate inheritance.

```
1 class myImmortalClass:
2     def getLifespan(self):
3         return "Immortal"
4
5 class myVampireClass(myImmortalClass):
6     subSpeciesName = 'Vampire'          # Class
variables are generally shared by all instances of a
class.
7
8     def __init__(self, name):
9         self._name = name
10
11    def greeting(self):
```

```
12          print(f"Hi! My name is {self._name} and I'm
a {self.subSpeciesName}. Lycans were made to serve us,
Humans to feed us.")
13
14 class myLycanClass(myImmortalClass):
15     subSpeciesName = 'Lycan'
16
17     def __init__(self, name):
18         print("myLycanClass has been invoked.") #
Notice that this method is invoked when a
myMichaelPostLycanBiteClass object is created.
19         self._name = name
20
21     def greeting(self):
22         print(f"Hi! My name is {self._name} and I'm
a {self.subSpeciesName}. No matter what any bat claims,
Lycans and Vampires are equals.")
23
24 class myMichaelPostLycanBiteClass(myLycanClass):
25
26     def salutation(self):
27         print(f"Hello! My name is {self._name}. I'm
~28 and a surgeon's intern. Please don't tell anyone
that I was recently bitten by a wolf.")
```

For now, we can take *myImmortalClass* as our base class. Its "children" are: *myVampireClass* and *myLycanClass*. Its "grandchild" is *myMichaelPostLycanBiteClass*. We don't have to explicitly define the *getLifespan()* method in its descendants. They all **inherit** it from the base class.

 Tip

The syntax for an inherited class in Python looks like this:

```
class nameOfClassThatInherits(name Of Class
  That It Inherits From):
    <statement 1>
```

```
        ...
        <statement n>
```

```
>>> vamp1 = myVampireClass("Viktor")
>>>
>>> vamp1.getLifespan()
'Immortal'
>>>
>>> wolf1 = myLycanClass("Lucian")
myLycanClass has been invoked.
>>>
>>> wolf1.getLifespan()
'Immortal'
>>>
>>> m1 = myMichaelPostLycanBiteClass("Michael Corvin")
myLycanClass has been invoked.
>>>
>>> m1.getLifespan()
'Immortal'
>>>
```

Attributes are also inherited from parent classes. Notice how the object *m1* inherits the subspecies attribute and *greeting()* from *myLycanClass*.

```
>>> m1.subSpeciesName
'Lycan'
>>>
>>> m1.greeting()
Hi! My name is Michael Corvin and I'm a Lycan. No matter
 what any bat claims, Lycans and Vampires are equals.
```

1.3.3. Overriding

To illustrate overriding let's go back to our Underworld example. Although Alexander Corvinus was immortal, he wasn't much stronger or faster than the average human. But his two sons were. Vampires are much stronger and faster than humans are, and Lycans surpass Vampires in both cases.

Please have a look at the code in *underworldclass1.py*!

```python
1 class myImmortalClass:
2     averageSpeed = 5
3     averageStrength = 5
4
5     def getLifespan(self):
6         return "Immortal"
7
8 class myVampireClass(myImmortalClass):
9     subSpeciesName = 'Vampire'
10     averageSpeed = 15
11     averageStrength = 15
12
13    def __init__(self, name):
14        self._name = name
15
16    def greeting(self):
17        print(f"Hi! My name is {self._name} and I'm
a {self.subSpeciesName}. Lycans were made to serve us,
Humans to feed us.")
18
19 class myLycanClass(myImmortalClass):
20     subSpeciesName = 'Lycan'
21     averageSpeed = 25
22     averageStrength = 25
23
24    def __init__(self, name):
25        self._name = name
26
27    def greeting(self):
28        print(f"Hi! My name is {self._name} and I'm
a {self.subSpeciesName}. No matter what any bat claims,
Lycans and Vampires are equals.")
29
30 class myMichaelPostLycanBiteClass(myLycanClass):
```

```
31      def __init__(self):
32          pass
33
34      def greeting(self):
35          print(f"Hello! My name is Michael Corvin.
    I'm ~24 and a surgeon's intern. Please don't tell
    anyone that I was recently bitten by a wolf.")
```

In unarmed combat between Viktor and Lucian, Lucian would most likely win. These
2 child classes inherit their strength and speed attributes from their parent class. But,
they **override** the parent values and each class has its own unique values.

```
>>> vamp1 = myVampireClass("Viktor")
>>>
>>> wolf1 = myLycanClass("Lucian")
>>>
>>> vamp1.averageStrength, vamp1.averageSpeed
(15, 15)
>>>
>>> wolf1.averageStrength, wolf1.averageSpeed
(25, 25)
```

In *underworldclass.py* class *myMichaelPostLycanBiteClass* inherited its *greeting()*
method from *myLycanClass*. Now, it overrides this method. When a child class explicitly implements a method or attribute whose name is identical to that found in its
parent class, Python uses the child implementation rather than the parent's.

Method Resolution Order(MRO) in Python is the order in which a method/attribute
is searched for in a class hierarchy. In the code shown below, which is found in *at-
tributesMRO.py*, which value of *subSpeciesName* should *myMichaelPostLycanBite-
Class* use?

```
1 class myImmortalClass:
2     subSpeciesName = 'Mutated human'
3
4 class myVampireClass(myImmortalClass):
5     subSpeciesName = 'Vampire'
```

```
 6
 7 class myLycanClass(myImmortalClass):
 8     subSpeciesName = 'Lycan'
 9
10 class myMichaelPostLycanBiteClass(myLycanClass):
11     heightInCm = 186
```

In a single inheritance situation, _mro_ will return a tuple of classes, starting from the bottom and moving up the class hierarchy to the base class.

```
>>> myMichaelPostLycanBiteClass.__mro__
(<class '__main__.myMichaelPostLycanBiteClass'>,
 <class '__main__.myLycanClass'>, <class
 '__main__.myImmortalClass'>, <class 'object'>)
>>>
```

A Unified Modeling Language(UML) diagram of this hierarchy is shown below. The arrows in the diagram go from child to parent.

Figure 1.1. UML diagram illustrating Single Inheritance

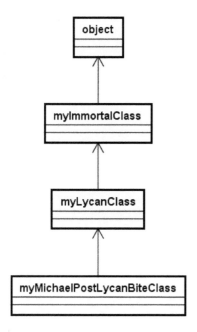

As you would expect, the parent of *myMichaelPostLycanBiteClass* is *myLycanClass* and so on. Thus, *myMichaelPostLycanBiteClass* uses the subspecies attribute from *myLycanClass*. But, what is the *object* class?

Most[2] classes in Python3 implicitly inherit from the root or superclass *object*. A lot of functionality, including the magic methods we have been overriding come from this superclass.

1.3.4. Multiple Inheritance

I will very briefly address multiple inheritance. This feature allows a class to inherit methods and attributes from more than one parent class.

Illustratory code can be found in *underworld-multi-class.py*.

---

[2]There are exceptions to this general rule, but, they go beyond the scope of this book.

Figure 1.2. UML diagram illustrating Multiple Inheritance

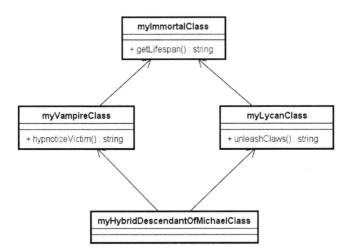

The vampires I know of from previous literature, sometimes have the ability to hypnotise their prey. Though I haven't come across any mention of this in the Underworld franchise, let's assume they too have this ability. The descendants of Michael have abilities that were otherwise unique to the subspecies of their forebears. Multiple inheritance allows us to express this relationship.

```
>>>
>>> e1 = myHybridDescendantOfMichaelClass('Eve')
>>>
>>> e1.greeting()
Hi! My name is Eve and I'm a Hybrid.
>>>
>>> e1.hypnotizeVictim()
Look into my eyes! You will do as I command...
>>>
>>> e1.unleashClaws()
My claws are strong enough to cut through steel. Clang,
 clang!
>>>
```

The declaration of *myHybridDescendantOfMichaelClass* happens on line 36 of *un-
derworld-multi-class.py*.

```
class myHybridDescendantOfMichaelClass(myVampireClass,
  myLycanClass):
```

The first argument, i.e. *myVampireClass* precedes *myLycanClass* in the MRO. Python
thus searches the vampire class first during method/attribute resolution.

```
>>>
>>> myHybridDescendantOfMichaelClass.__mro__
(<class '__main__.myHybridDescendantOfMichaelClass'>,
 <class '__main__.myVampireClass'>,
 <class '__main__.myLycanClass'>, <class
 '__main__.myImmortalClass'>, <class 'object'>)
>>>
```

Flipping these arguments around changes the MRO.

```
>>>
>>> myHybridDescendantOfMichaelClass.__mro__
(<class '__main__.myHybridDescendantOfMichaelClass'>,
 <class '__main__.myLycanClass'>, <class
 '__main__.myVampireClass'>, <class
 '__main__.myImmortalClass'>, <class 'object'>)
>>>
```

The first PyQt script you'll encounter in this book has a *super()* method. Many PyQt
scripts also use this method. What does it do?

1.3.5. *super()*-Man

super() usually[3] goes to the subsequent class in the current classes' MRO, and attempts to resolve whatever method/attribute we're interested in there.

Have a look at the following code found in *super101.py*!

---

[3]As you've probably come to expect by now, there are exceptions to this general rule.

```
 1 class myBaseClass:
 2      def __init__(self):
 3          print("myBaseClass.__init__ called")
 4
 5 class myChildClass1(myBaseClass):
 6      def __init__(self):
 7          myBaseClass.__init__(self)
 8          print("myChildClass1.__init__ called")
 9
10 class myChildClass2(myBaseClass):
11      def __init__(self):
12          myBaseClass.__init__(self)
13          print("myChildClass2.__init__ called")
14
15 class myGrandChildClass(myChildClass1,
   myChildClass2):
16      def __init__(self):
17          myChildClass1.__init__(self)
18          myChildClass2.__init__(self)
19          print("myGrandChildClass.__init__ called")
```

When we create a *myChildClass1* object we get the following output:

```
>>> x = myChildClass1()
myBaseClass.__init__ called
myChildClass1.__init__ called
>>>
```

The script behaves predictably in a single-inheritance scenario. The result of creating a *myGrandChildClass* object is shown below.

```
>>>
>>> y = myGrandChildClass()
myBaseClass.__init__ called
myChildClass1.__init__ called
myBaseClass.__init__ called
myChildClass2.__init__ called
```

```
myGrandChildClass.__init__ called
>>>
```

myBaseClass.__init__ has been called twice. This can cause a problem when a child class sets program state(State in a program is a list of variables and their values) and then an invocation of the parent method resets changed variables back to their default state.

To remedy this we use *super()*. When the interpreter "sees" *super()*, it goes to the next class in the MRO. In a way, the child classes pass the buck. If each class consistently uses *super()* and only calls it once, the entire MRO will be stepped through and each method will only be called once. Have a look at *fixed-super.py* for an example of this!

```
1 class myBaseClass:
2     def __init__(self):
3         print("myBaseClass.__init__ called")
4
5 class myChildClass1(myBaseClass):
6     def __init__(self):
7         super().__init__()
8         print("myChildClass1.__init__ called")
9
10 class myChildClass2(myBaseClass):
11     def __init__(self):
12         super().__init__()
13         print("myChildClass2.__init__ called")
14
15 class myGrandChildClass(myChildClass1,
myChildClass2):
16     def __init__(self):
17         super().__init__()
18         print("myGrandChildClass.__init__ called")
```

When we use *super()* we don't need to pass self as an argument. This time *myBaseClass.__init__* is only called once.

```
>>> y = myGrandChildClass()
```

```
myBaseClass.__init__ called
myChildClass2.__init__ called
myChildClass1.__init__ called
myGrandChildClass.__init__ called
>>>
```

 Note

Although *super()* is often invoked in calls to *_init_*(), it can be used with other methods.

1.4. Summary

Python is marketed as a beginner-friendly programming language. Although it's possible to perform complicated tasks using two or three lines of code, there is often some ambiguity/inconsistency that even experienced users ignore or don't know about. To add insult to injury, newbie coders are introduced to OOP right off the bat.

And yet many colleges and high schools introduce students to programming using Python.

My humble opinion is that Python should not be taught as a first programming language. To those who will be introduced to programming via Python, I salute you!

1.5. References

- https://en.wikipedia.org/wiki/Docstring
- https://en.wikipedia.org/wiki/Finalizer
- https://docs.python.org/3/tutorial/classes.html#a-first-look-at-classes
- https://blog.gougousis.net/oop-inheritance-what-when-and-why/

This page inten-
tionally left blank

Chapter 2. Your first PyQt programs

As at the time of writing this (June 2024), the latest version of Python is version 3.12.4. However, any version of Python 3 should work.

 Note

If you have both python2 and python3 on your system, you'll need to be careful about which one you invoke when compiling a program. Those with both versions of python may need to specifically invoke *python3*. If you only have python3 installed, typing *python* at compile time will be sufficient. Since I have both, I will use *python3*.

If you're using pip to install PyQt6 and various other packages, it may be a good idea to upgrade it to the latest version. For more details go to: https://pip.pypa.io/en/stable/installation/

If you have both python2 and python3 installed, *pip* usually manages Python2 packages, while *pip3* is used for Python3 packages.

Open a command prompt and type the following:

```
pip3 install pyqt6-tools
```

This command will install PyQt6 and some tools that you will need later on.

If you want to follow along, you can create a new text file and paste in the following code. Else, this and all other code will be found in the source code that came with your book. The code for each chapter is in a folder named after that chapter.

2.1. First example

In the folder for this chapter, open a file named *simple.py*.

```
1 from PyQt6.QtWidgets import QApplication, QWidget ❶
2 import sys ❷
3
```

```
 4 class MainWindow(QWidget): 3
 5     def __init__(self): 4
 6         super().__init__() 5
 7         self.initUI() 6
 8
 9     def initUI(self):
10         self.setWindowTitle('Simple example 1') 7
11         self.resize(230, 254) 8
12         self.show() 9
13
14
15 if __name__ == '__main__':        10
16     qApp = QApplication(sys.argv) 11
17     w = MainWindow() 12
18     sys.exit(qApp.exec()) 13
```

1 2 These lines import the modules needed to run the script. The function *exit()* that we'll later use to terminate our script is part of the *sys* module.

10   When the Python interpreter reads a source file, it executes all the code found in it.

Before executing the code, it will define a few special variables. For example, if the Python interpreter is running the source file as the main program, it sets the special __*name*__ variable to have the value __*main*__ . If this file is being imported from another module, __*name*__ will be set to the module's name.

In the case of our script, let's assume that it's executing as the main function, i.e. you type something like

python3 simple.py

on the command line. After setting up the special variables, it will execute the *import* statement and load the modules specified in lines 1 and 2. It will then interpret the *if* statement and see that __*name*__ does equal '__*main*__', so it will execute the block in lines 16-18. Line 15 allows us to intercept the interpreter execution flow and harness it for our own ends.

Please see Appendix D for a more detailed explanation!

11   Every PyQt application must contain an instance of the application object. The *sys.argv* parameter contains a list of arguments passed to the script from the command line. In our case we didn't pass any arguments to our script.

12   We instantiate an object called *w* from the *MainWindow* class. The *MainWindow* class contains all the functionality of our simple app.

13   We enter the main loop of the application. In programs with UI(user interface) components, whatever happens in the program for example if we resize the main window, drag objects into the main window etc is determined by actions the user makes.

Line 18 ensures that the execution flow loops infinitely while "listening" for user input. The event we're most interested in is the exit event, that is, when the user closes the main window. We pass this to our script as its cue to terminate our script.

So far we have looked at the script initialization boilerplate of a typical PyQt program. Now we examine the most important part of our simple script.

3   Here we define our main class which inherits from the *QWidget* class. This is why *QWidget* is passed as an argument to our class.

4   We define the *__init__()* method of our class.

5   As explained in the previous chapter, *super()* fetches the subsequent class in the current classes' MRO(Method Resolution Order). Once we have this class, we call its *__init__()* method. This allows PyQt to perform its default initialization on our widgets.

6   We call the *initUI()* method. All our UI initialization is done in this method.

7   All UI components we interact with in PyQt, for example buttons, sliders, drop-down menus etc are called widgets. The base class for all UI objects in PyQt is called *QWidget*. Our widget in this example is our main window. We set the window title by calling the *setWindowTitle()* method and passing it the text we want to use as an argument.

8   The *resize()* method simply sets the size of a widget. We set a size of 230 pixels width and 254 pixels height.

9   We display our widget on screen by calling the *show()* method.

To run the program switch to the directory where the script is contained in your CLI. Type in the command:

python3 simple.py

Your output should look similar to the following:

Figure 2.1. Your first PyQt app

2.2. Second example

Look at the top-left hand corner of the illustration above! This is the generic icon which shows up in scripts run on Windows. You'll learn how to set up your own icon in the following script.

Open the file named *simple1.py*. Most of the code in this example was covered in the previous example. Let's go through what's new together.

```
11      def initUI(self):
12          self.setWindowTitle('Simple example 2')
13
14          self.setWindowIcon(QIcon('240px-
Smiley.svg.png')) ❶
15
16          btnClick = QPushButton(parent=self) ❷
17          #btnClick = QPushButton(self)
18          #btnClick = QPushButton()
19          btnClick.setText('Quit') ❸
20          btnClick.move(110, 50) ❹
21          btnClick.clicked.connect(QApplication.
instance() .quit) ❺
22
```

```
23            self.resize(300, 254)
24            self.show()
```

1   We set an icon for our application. The *setWindowIcon()* method expects a *QI-con* object as its argument. Of course, the file specified must exist or else Qt will fall back on the generic icon for your operating system.

2   Here we create a button widget.

It's important to note that a widget without a parent widget is always an independent window, called a top-level widget. In the previous example, we worked exclusively with a top-level widget. Methods like *setWindowTitle()* and *setWindowIcon()* are only available to top-level widgets.

Non-top-level widgets are child widgets displayed within their parent widgets. Most widgets in Qt are mainly useful as child widgets. For example, it is possible to display a button as a top-level window, but most people prefer to put their buttons inside other widgets like we're doing on line 15.

You can declare a child widget like we have here on line 15 or you can do it as shown on line 16. Line 15 explicitly sets the parent argument, while PyQt is able to infer the parent argument on its own as shown on line 16.

Please note that if you don't specify a parent for this widget, then it won't be visible on screen! Comment line 15 and uncomment line 17 to see this as illustrated in Figure 1.3.

3   We set the text property of our button. This is the text that will be seen on the surface of our button.

4   We position our button relative to our parent widget. The top-left of our window has the coordinates (0, 0). The x coordinate increases the further right we move, the y coordinate increases the further down we move, both to a maximum at the bottom-right corner of the window. The coordinates we used i.e. (110,50), specify the top-left corner of our button widget.

5   Here we set up code to handle user clicks on the button.

Android, Swift and many other "visual" programming languages, have callback functions to handle input events. Qt uses a signal and slot mechanism to handle input events.

In our case, a signal is emitted when the user clicks on the button we've created. A slot is code that processes this signal. A slot can point to a Python function or another slot.

The emitted signal is connected to the *quit* method which terminates the application. Communication is done between two objects: the sender and the receiver. The sender is the push button, the receiver is the application object.

Signals will be covered in greater depth in a later chapter.

To run the program, switch to the directory where the script is contained in your CLI. Type in the command:

python3 simple1.py

Your output should look similar to the following:

Figure 2.2. Second example

Figure 2.3. Parentless button

2.3. Summary

This chapter walked you through installing PyQt as well as the basics of some very simple PyQt apps.

There is already a problem though: run *simple1.py* again to see it. The app as shown in Figure 1.2 has the button positioned roughly at the horizontal center of the screen. When you maximize the parent window, the button is pushed towards the top-left of the parent window. Try it for yourself and confirm this! The next chapter will teach you how to preserve widget positions regardless of parent window size.

This page inten-
tionally left blank

Chapter 3. Layout management in PyQt

Layout management refers to the manner in which we position widgets on the application window. We can position our widgets using absolute positioning or with layout classes.

3.1. Absolute positioning

This is how we've positioned widgets so far. It has the following limitations:

- As shown before, the size and position of widgets don't change when we resize the parent window.
- Applications may look different on various platforms.
- If we change anything, we have to readjust the position of our widgets. Precious developer time is wasted getting everything just right.

The code below is contained in a file named *position.py* in the folder for this chapter.

```
15 label1 = QLabel(parent=self) 1
16 label1.setText('Don\'t')
17 label1.move(80, 50)
18
19 label2 = QLabel(self) 2
20 label2.setText('use')
21 label2.move(90, 80)
22
23 label3 = QLabel('this positioning technique in real
life!',self) 3
24 label3.move(100, 110)
```

1 2 3 *QLabel* is used for displaying text or an image. Lines 15, 19, 23 show different ways of constructing the *QLabel* widget. Just like with our *QPushButton* instance from the previous chapter, if we don't pass any arguments to *QLabel*, then it will not be visible.

We position the labels by providing x and y Cartesian coordinates. The top-left corner of the parent window has coordinates (0,0) while the bottom-right corner has the maximum x and y coordinate values.

Figure 3.1. Absolute positioning

3.2. Layout classes

The Qt API(Application programming interface) provides layout classes for elegant management of widget positioning inside the container. The advantages of layout managers over absolute positioning are:

- Widgets inside the window are automatically resized when the amount of available space for them changes.
- Ensures uniform appearance on display devices with different resolutions.
- Adding or removing widgets dynamically without having to redesign is possible.

PyQt has 4 layout managers that we'll cover in this chapter:

- Box layout. This is further subdivided into two.
- Grid layout.
- Form layout.

A layout manager is like a container. We add our widgets into this container in the order we want them to be displayed, then we pass our container to our top-level widget.

3.2.1. Box layout

This layout is represented in Qt using the *QBoxLayout* class. This class lines up its widgets vertically or horizontally. Its derived classes are *QVBoxLayout* (for arranging widgets vertically) and *QHBoxLayout* (for arranging widgets horizontally).

Important

A derived class is a class that inherits or derives from another existing class.

The code below is contained in a file named *position1.py* in the chapter folder.

```
 9 def initUI(self):
10   self.setWindowTitle('Box layout1')
11
12   btn1 = QPushButton("Button 1", self) ❶
13   btn2 = QPushButton("Button 2", self) ❷
14
15   vbox = QVBoxLayout() ❸
16   vbox.addWidget(btn1) ❹
17   vbox.addStretch() ❺
18   vbox.addWidget(btn2)
19   self.setLayout(vbox) ❻
```

❶ ❷ These create two buttons and specify the text on them.

❸   A *QVBoxLayout* class lines up widgets vertically.

❹   Widgets inside a layout are displayed in the order in which they're added. Our layout will have 1 column with 3 rows. Line 16 adds *btn1* to the first row of the column.

❺   This adds a stretch factor or stretchable empty space between the two buttons.

❻   We set the layout of the main window.

Two buttons and a stretch factor are stacked vertically in the main window. The stretch factor will automatically take up the empty space between the two button widgets and the layout will ensure a consistent look on different window sizes.

Figure 3.2. Vertical box layout

3.2.1.1. Second example

The code below is contained in a file named *position2.py* in the chapter folder. *QH-BoxLayout* is used to stack the widgets horizontally from left-to-right.

```
 9 def initUI(self):
10   self.setWindowTitle('Box layout2')
11
12   btn1 = QPushButton("Button 1", self)
13   btn2 = QPushButton("Button 2", self)
14
15   hbox = QHBoxLayout()
16   hbox.addWidget(btn1)
17   hbox.addStretch()
18   hbox.addWidget(btn2)
19   self.setLayout(hbox)
```

Figure 3.3. Horizontal box layout

3.2.1.2. Third example

The code below is contained in a file named *position3.py* in the chapter folder.

```
 9 def initUI(self):
10   self.setWindowTitle('Box layout3')
11
12   btn1 = QPushButton("Button 1", self)
13   btn2 = QPushButton("Button 2", self)
14
15   vbox = QVBoxLayout()
16   vbox.addWidget(btn1)
17   vbox.addStretch()
18   vbox.addWidget(btn2)
19
20   btn3 = QPushButton("Button 3", self)
21   btn4 = QPushButton("Button 4", self)
22
23   hbox = QHBoxLayout()
24   hbox.addWidget(btn3)
25   hbox.addStretch()
26   hbox.addWidget(btn4)
27
```

```
28  vbox.addStretch()
29  vbox.addLayout(hbox)
30
31  self.setLayout(vbox)
```

This example demonstrates nesting(i.e. one inside another) of layouts. First, two buttons with a stretchable empty space between them are added to a vertical box layout.
Then, a horizontal box layout object with two buttons and a stretchable empty space
is added to it. Finally, the vertical box layout object is applied to the top-level widget
using the *setLayout()* method.

Figure 3.4. Horizontal and vertical combined

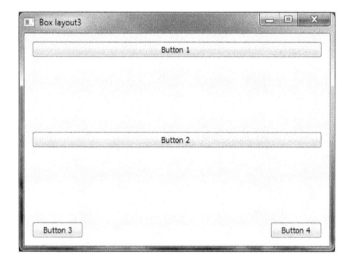

3.2.2. Grid layout

This layout is represented in Qt using the *QGridLayout* class. It is a grid of cells
arranged in rows and columns. Position 0,0 is at the top-left corner of the grid. Position
x increases the further right we move, y increases the further down we move. The
code below is contained in a file named *position4.py*.

```
11 def initUI(self):
12  self.setWindowTitle('Grid layout')
13
14  label1 = QLabel(self)
```

```
15  label1.setPixmap(QPixmap("Smiley_green_alien.svg.
png")) 1
16  label2 = QLabel(self)
17  label2.setPixmap(QPixmap("Smiley_green_alien_
wow .svg.png"))
18  label3 = QLabel(self)
19  label3.setPixmap(QPixmap("Smiley_green_alien_black
_ninja .svg.png"))
20  label4 = QLabel(self)
21  label4.setPixmap(QPixmap("Smiley_green_alien_big
_eyes .svg.png"))
22
23  grid = QGridLayout()
24  grid.addWidget(label1, 0, 0) 2
25  grid.addWidget(label2, 1, 0)
26  grid.addWidget(label3, 0, 1)
27  grid.addWidget(label4, 1, 1)
28
29  self.setLayout(grid)
```

1   It was mentioned earlier that *QLabel* can display text or an image. Here, the *setPixmap()* method is used to point to this image. It accepts an argument of type *QPixmap*, so we pass a *QPixmap* object with the name of our image file as its constructor.

The label object adjusts its size depending on the size of the *QPixmap* image.

2   Lines 24-27 put each label in a grid cell.

Figure 3.5. Grid layout example

3.2.3. Form layout

This layout is represented in Qt using the *QFormLayout* class. This class lays out its children in a two-column form. The left column consists of labels and the right column consists of form field widgets e.g. line editors, spin boxes, etc.

The code below is contained in a file named *position5.py*.

```
10 def initUI(self):
11   self.setWindowTitle('Form layout')
12
13   nameLineEdit = QLineEdit() ❶
14   passwordLineEdit = QLineEdit() ❷
15   emailLineEdit = QLineEdit() ❸
16   ageSpinBox = QSpinBox() ❹
17
18   passwordLineEdit.setEchoMode(QLineEdit.EchoMode.
Password)
19
```

```
20   formLayout = QFormLayout() 5
21   formLayout.addRow("Name:", nameLineEdit)
22   formLayout.addRow("Password:", passwordLineEdit)
23   formLayout.addRow("Email:", emailLineEdit)
24   formLayout.addRow("Age:", ageSpinBox)
25
26   self.setLayout(formLayout)
```

1 2 We create three line edit fields. The *QLineEdit* widget is a one-line text editor. It
3   allows the user to enter and edit a single line of plain text with a useful collection
       of editing functions, including undo and redo, cut and paste, as well as drag and
       drop.
       By changing its *echoMode()* property, it can also be used as a "write-only" field,
       for inputs such as passwords.

4   We create a spin box widget. The *QSpinBox* class provides a spin box widget.
       It is designed to handle integers and discrete sets of values (e.g. month names).
       QSpinBox allows the user to choose a value by clicking the up/down buttons
       or pressing up/down on the keyboard to increase/decrease the value currently
       displayed. The user can also type the value in manually. The spin box supports
       integer values but can also be extended to use different strings with *validate()*,
       textFromValue() and *valueFromText()*.

5   Look at the figure below! To create such a layout, we'd have needed to create
       a vertical layout and nested four horizontal layout widgets inside it. Instead, by
       using *QFormLayout* each horizontal widget is added as a row. And we don't
       need to create label widgets, since this is automatically done for us. All we do
       is specify the text on the label plus its corresponding field element.

Figure 3.6. Form layout

3.3. Summary

This chapter covered the basics of layout management. We briefly touched on event handling in the first chapter. The next chapter will further explore this topic.

3.4. References

- https://doc.qt.io/qt-6/qlabel.html#pixmap-prop
- https://doc-snapshots.qt.io/qt6-dev/qhboxlayout.html
- https://doc.qt.io/qt-6/qvboxlayout.html
- https://doc-snapshots.qt.io/qt6-dev/qformlayout.html
- https://doc.qt.io/qt-6/qspinbox.html
- https://doc-snapshots.qt.io/qt6-dev/qlineedit.html

Chapter 4. Signals and slots

As mentioned in chapter one, Qt uses a signal and slot mechanism to handle input events. A signal is emitted when something of potential interest happens. A slot is a Python callable(think of this as a function). If a signal is connected to a slot, then the slot is called when the signal is emitted. If a signal isn't connected then nothing happens.

For example, the spinbox in *position5.py*(of the Chapter 2 folder) emits a signal whenever you move the slider up or down. But since it wasn't connected to a slot, Qt ignores the signal.

In addition to notifying Qt that the spin box has been clicked on, the spin object also passes data about the current value of the spin box. Usually as a coder all you're interested in is the click event. The code listing below shows you how to use this extra data in case you ever need it.

4.1. Custom slot

The code below is contained in a file named *signals.py* in the chapter folder. Run the script and pay close attention to your CLI window. When you click the up or down arrows on the spin box, the current value of the spin box is printed to your CLI.

Tip

A full-size image of the following screenshot can be found in the *images* folder.

Figure 4.1. Custom slot demo

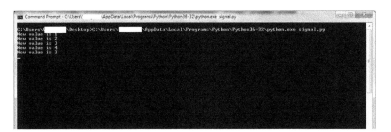

We import the module we need in order to use the *pyqtSlot* decorator on line 2. For more information on decorators see: https://gist.github.com/ Zearin/2f40b7b9cfc51132851a.

```
1 from PyQt6.QtWidgets import QApplication, QWidget,
QFormLayout, QSpinBox, QLineEdit
2 from PyQt6.QtCore import pyqtSlot
3 import sys
```

```
19              formLayout.addRow("Age:", ageSpinBox)
20
21              ageSpinBox.valueChanged[int].connect(self.
headsUp) 1
22
23              self.setLayout(formLayout)
24
25              self.show()
26
27      @pyqtSlot(int) 2
28      def headsUp(self, arg1): 3
29              print("New value is", arg1) 4
30
31 if __name__ == '__main__':
```

1   As explained in the documentation for *QSpinBox*(link is in the references section), this widget can emit a value changed signal that contains integer data. Line 23 shows PyQt syntax for registering a slot for this signal and its data.

2   Although PyQt allows any Python callable to be used as a slot when connecting signals, it is sometimes necessary to explicitly mark a Python method as being a Qt slot and provide a C++ signature for it. PyQt provides the *pyqtSlot()* function decorator to do this. Line 29 declares a slot that processes integer values. Every time the value of the widget changes, a signal with the new spinbox value is emitted.

3   We declare a function that will take one integer parameter called *arg1*.

4   We print our value on the command console.

4.2. Using a provided slot

The previous example showed you how to create a custom slot to process widget signals. However, most widgets already come with some slots built in.

The code below is contained in a file named *signals1.py*.

```
 9 def initUI(self):
10   self.setWindowTitle('Signals example1')
11
12   lcd = QLCDNumber(self) 1
13   dial = QDial(self) 2
14   dial.setMinimum(50) 3
15
16   vbox = QVBoxLayout()
17   vbox.addWidget(lcd)
18   vbox.addWidget(dial)
19
20   self.setLayout(vbox)
21   dial.valueChanged.connect(lcd.display) 4
```

1 2 We display a *QDial* which looks like a knob on an analogue device and a *QL-CDNumber* display widget. *QDial* is used when the user needs to control a value within a program-definable range, and the range wraps around (for example, with angles measured from 0 to 359 degrees). The *QLCDNumber* widget displays a number using LCD-like digits.

3   We set a minimum value for our dial.

4   We connect the *valueChanged* signal of the slider to the display slot of the LCD widget. This inbuilt slot will display whatever value is pointed at and emitted as a signal by the dial.

When you first run the script, the LCD will display a default value of 0.

Figure 4.2. The LCD widget displays its default value

When you move the slider **slightly**, a signal is sent to the LCD which sets its minimum value to 50.

Figure 4.3. The LCD widget displays a new value based on the dial minimum

4.3. A typical example

Usually, all you're interested in is the click event. The example below typifies the pattern in most of the PyQt scripts you'll encounter. Its code is contained in a file named *signals2.py*.

```
20   vbox.addWidget(self.submitButton)
21
22   self.submitButton.clicked.connect(self.
submitContact) 1
23
24   self.setLayout(vbox)
25   self.show()
26
27 def submitContact(self):
28   name = self.nameLineEdit.text() 2
29
30   if name == "": 3
31     QMessageBox.critical(self, "Empty Field",
32           "Please enter a name!") 4
33   else:
34     QMessageBox.information(self, "Success!",
35           "Hello %s!" % name)
```

1   Most of this code is familiar to you. We nest a form layout inside a vertical box layout. Line 22 forwards the click signal on the button to the *submitContact()* method.

2   We're inside the *submitContact()* method. We retrieve the value of the line edit widget and assign it to a variable called *name*.

3 4 If the line edit widget is blank we issue an error message. The first parameter on line 31 i.e. *self* refers to the parent window. The second is the text shown in the title of the message box. The third parameter is the main text of the message box. We show a message box with a critical severity level.

Important

The *QMessageBox* class provides a modal dialog for informing the user or, for asking the user a question and receiving an answer. It has four predefined message severity levels, or message types, which really only differ in the predefined icon they each show. These are:

1. **Question**: For asking a question during normal operations.
2. **Information**: For reporting information about normal operations.
3. **Warning**: For reporting non-critical errors.

4. **Critical**: For reporting critical errors.

Figure 4.4. Your first interactive app

4.4. Summary

This chapter introduced PyQt signals and slots to you. Interacting with your users will usually be the core of your PyQt apps and signals will help you with this. Most widgets provide easy to use signals and slots. The Qt documentation will be a great help as you write more complex apps.

4.5. References

- https://doc.qt.io/qt-6/qspinbox.html#valueChanged
- https://doc.qt.io/qt-6/qabstractslider.html#minimum-prop
- https://doc.qt.io/qt-6/qmessagebox.html#details
- https://www.riverbankcomputing.com/static/Docs/PyQt6/signals_slots.html

Chapter 5. PyQt widgets

Let's review some widgets you're likely to encounter while coding with PyQt.

5.1. QLineEdit

By now, you're well acquainted with this one. The *QLineEdit* widget is a one-line text editor. A line edit allows the user to enter and edit a single line of plain text with a useful collection of editing functions, including undo and redo, cut-and-paste, as well as drag and drop.

Have a look at the following snippet from *widget.py*!

```
19  self.resultLabel.move(10,150)
20
21  basicLineEdit.textChanged[str].connect(self.
headsUp) 1
22
23  self.resize(300, 300)
24  self.show()
25
26 @pyqtSlot(str) 2
27 def headsUp(self, arg1):
28  self.resultLabel.setText(arg1) 3
29  self.resultLabel.adjustSize() 4
```

1   We connect the *textChanged* signal emitted by the widget to our slot. Any time you alter the text within a *QLineEdit*, this signal is emitted. The emitted signal has an argument of type string, which contains the text contained in the widget.

2   We declare a slot that processes values of type string. Behind the scenes, Qt monitors our widget. If the value contained in it changes, it emits a signal with this new value. The signal emitted is set to contain a string representation of the latest widget contents.

3   We take the value of the line edit widget and set it as the text for the label.

4   This will adjust the width of the label widget to match the text contained in it. It's quite possible for a *QLabel* widget to contain more text than is displayed

on its face. Don't believe me? Un-comment line 18 and run the app again! The label will only display 100 pixels of text.

Figure 5.1. QLineEdit example

5.2. QCalendarWidget

The *QCalendarWidget* class provides a monthly based calendar widget allowing the user to select a date. By default, the current date is selected, and the user can select another date using both mouse and keyboard. The calendar grid is not visible by default.

If we select a date on the widget, a *clicked* signal is emitted. The code contained in *widget1.py* connects this signal to our custom slot.

```
16   calendar = QCalendarWidget(self)
17   calendar.setGridVisible(True) ❶
18   calendar.clicked[QDate].connect(self.headsUp)
19
20   self.resultLabel =
QLabel(calendar.selectedDate().toString(), self) ❷
21
22   vbox.addWidget(calendar)
23   vbox.addWidget(self.resultLabel)
24
```

```
25  self.resize(300, 300)
26  self.show()
27
28  @pyqtSlot(QDate)
29  def headsUp(self, arg1):
30    self.resultLabel.setText(arg1.toString()) ▣
```

1   This enables the calendar grid.

2   *calendar.selectedDate()* returns an object of type *QDate*. Since the label widget only accepts string objects, we call the *toString()* method of *QDate* to convert the output into a format acceptable by our label widget.

3   When we select any date on our calendar, a signal containing the chosen date is emitted. We capture that date and display it on our label.

Figure 5.2. QCalendarWidget example

5.3. QCheckBox

A *QCheckBox* is an option button that can be switched on (checked) or off (unchecked). Checkboxes are typically used to represent features in an application that can be enabled or disabled.

Whenever a checkbox is checked or cleared, it emits the signal *stateChanged()*. The code contained in *widget2.py* connects to this signal. We use it to toggle the grid on the calendar widget.

```
18   self.calendar.clicked[QDate].connect(self.
headsUpCalendar)
19
20   checkbox = QCheckBox('Disable Grid?', self) 1
21   #checkbox.stateChanged.connect(self.
toggleCalendarGrid)
22   checkbox.stateChanged.connect(self.
headsUpCheckBox) 2
23
24   self.resultLabel =
QLabel(self.calendar.selectedDate().toString(), self)
25
26   vbox.addWidget(checkbox)
27   vbox.addWidget(self.calendar)
28   vbox.addWidget(self.resultLabel)
29
30   self.resize(300, 300)
31   self.show()
32
33 @pyqtSlot(QDate)
34 def headsUpCalendar(self, arg1):
35   self.resultLabel.setText(arg1.toString())
36
37 @pyqtSlot()
38 def headsUpCheckBox(self):
39   if not (self.calendar.isGridVisible()): 3
40     self.calendar.setGridVisible(True) 4
41   else:
42     self.calendar.setGridVisible(False) 5
```

1   We construct the checkbox widget and set its text.
2   We connect the *stateChanged()* signal to our slot.
3 4 By default the calendar grid is enabled. If the user checks the checkbox, the grid
        will be disabled if it's currently enabled.
5   Vice-versa.

Figure 5.3. Programmatically toggle the calendar grid

Instead of using a slot, we can also use a callback function to produce similar output. The function *toggleCalendarGrid()* in *widget2.py* demonstrates this. When you're not interested in processing parameters from our widgets, one may use a callback. The PyQt documentation at:

https://www.riverbankcomputing.com/static/Docs/PyQt6/ signals_slots.html#the-pyqtslot-decorator

indicates that slots reduce the amount of memory used and are faster.

5.4. QSlider

The QSlider widget provides a vertical or horizontal slider. The slider is the classic widget for controlling a bounded value. It lets the user move a slider handle along a horizontal or vertical groove and translates the handle's position into an integer value within the legal range.

By default the slider is oriented vertically:

Figure 5.4. Default slider orientation

The code contained in *widget3.py* will show you how to change the slider orientation. We use a slider together with a *QLCDNumber* widget to simulate a radio tuner.

```
14   slider = QSlider(self)
15   slider.setOrientation(Qt.Orientation. Horizontal) ❶
16   self.lcd.setProperty("value", 87.5) ❷
17
18   vbox = QVBoxLayout()
19   vbox.addWidget(self.lcd)
20   vbox.addWidget(slider)
21
22   self.setLayout(vbox)
23   slider.valueChanged[int].connect(self. headsUp) ❸
24
25   self.resize(300, 254)
26   self.show()
27
28 @pyqtSlot(int)
29 def headsUp(self, arg1):
30   display = str(87.5 + (0.207070707*arg1)) ❹
31   self.lcd.setProperty("value", display)
```

1 As mentioned earlier, the default slider orientation is vertical. The slider widgets alternate orientation can be set using the *setOrientation()* method as shown here. We pass it an enumeration with the value of *Qt.Orientation.Horizontal*.

2 This demonstrates setting the default display value for the LCD widget.

3 The slider emits a *valueChanged* signal when its value has changed. The default slider range is between 0 and 99. Whenever you move this slider, it calculates how far within its range you've moved it and emits a signal containing its new position(as an integer) within the range. Please note that the slider can only handle integer values! We take advantage of that in our custom slot.

4 Many countries use an FM broadcast band range of 87.5 to 108 MHz. Subtract 87.5 from 108 to get 20.5. Then divide that by 99 to get a step size of 0.207070707. Every time you shift the slider, the script takes its current position between 0 and 99 and calculates the corresponding frequency using the formula shown on this line.

Figure 5.5. Radio tuner simulation

5.5. QProgressBar

The *QProgressBar* widget provides a horizontal(by default) or vertical progress bar. The progress bar uses the concept of steps. You set it up by specifying the minimum and maximum possible step values, and it will display the percentage of steps that have been completed when you later give it the current step value.

The default minimum is 0, default maximum is 99 and the default step size is 1. *QProgressBar* utilizes animation to give the illusion of ticking away.

The code contained in *widget4.py* simulates a download or file transfer progress bar.

```
14   self.timerButton.clicked.connect(self.download)
15
16   self.progressBar = QProgressBar(self) ❶
17   self.progressBar.setGeometry(10, 20, 290, 25) ❷
18
19   self.timerButton.move(110,150)
20   self.progressBar.move(10,100)
21
22   self.resize(300, 300)
23   self.show()
24
25 def download(self):
26   self.completed = 0
27   self.timerButton.setEnabled(False) ❸
28
29   while self.completed < 15: ❹
30     self.completed += 1
31     time.sleep(1)
32     self.progressBar.setValue(self.completed)
```

❶ ❷ We initialize our progress bar widget. We also set its dimensions by specifying its top-left and bottom-right corners.

❹ We sleep for a second and then move the progress bar forward by 1%.

❸ We disable the button while we're in a loop.

Figure 5.6. QProgressBar demo

5.6. QOpenGLWidget

QOpenGLWidget provides functionality for displaying OpenGL graphics integrated into a Qt application. It is very simple to use: Make your class, inherit from it and use the subclass like any other *QWidget*, except that you have the choice between using *QPainter* and standard OpenGL rendering commands.

QOpenGLWidget provides three convenient virtual functions that you can re-implement in your subclass to perform the typical OpenGL tasks:
1. *paintGL()* - Renders the OpenGL scene. Gets called whenever the widget needs to be updated.
2. *resizeGL()* - Sets up the OpenGL viewport, projection, etc. Gets called whenever the widget has been resized (and also when it is shown for the first time, because all newly created widgets get a resize event automatically).
3. *initializeGL()* - Sets up the OpenGL resources and state. Gets called once before *resizeGL()* or *paintGL()* are called.

A comprehensive overview of OpenGL is beyond the scope of this document. Our focus will be on the interaction of this widget with PyQt. An app in a later chapter will use this widget(although it won't use any OpenGL code). A good beginner guide from the developers of OpenGL can be found at:
https://www.khronos.org/opengl/wiki/Getting_Started

> ### Tip
>
> You'll probably need to install PyOpenGL to get the code below to run.
> Run the following command to install it:
>
> *pip3 install PyOpenGL PyOpenGL_accelerate*
>
> See:
>
> http://pyopengl.sourceforge.net/documentation/installation.html
> for more details.
>
> For Windows users, you may refer to Appendix C for instructions on
> how to run this app using Docker.

The code contained in *widget5.py* draws a cube using OpenGL.

> ### Important
>
> If you get the following error message while running *widget5.py*, you
> probably need to install GLUT(OpenGL Utility Toolkit) or FreeGLUT
> on your system.
>
> ```
> OpenGL.error.NullFunctionError: Attempt to call
>  an undefined function glutInitDisplayMode,
>  check for bool(glutInitDisplayMode) before
>  calling
> ```

```
 5 try:
 6     from OpenGL import GL
 7 except ImportError:
 8     app = QApplication(sys.argv)
 9     QMessageBox.critical(None, "OpenGL check",
10             "PyOpenGL must be installed to run this
example.")
11     sys.exit(1)
12
13 from OpenGL.GL import * 2
14 from OpenGL.GLUT import * 3
15 from OpenGL.GLU import * 4
```

1 This try-except block will ensure that PyOpenGL is installed on your system. If
   not, then the app will exit with an error.

2 3 These modules provide the OpenGL functionality we will need.

4

**Line 43 executes the initialization method of our class. As soon as this executes,
control flow switches to *initializeGL()* then *resizeGL()*, then *paintGL()* and back to
initializeGL() again. Examine the output of the print statements on your terminal
to confirm this.**

```
43      def __init__(self, parent):
44          super(MainWindow, self).__init__(parent)
45          self.setMinimumSize(300, 300)
```

Figure 5.7. Output of the QOpenGLWidget demo on Linux

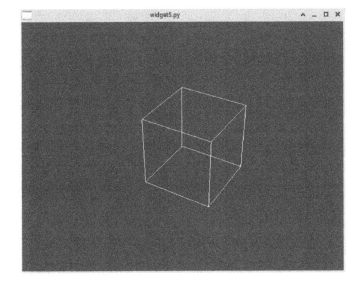

5.7. Miscellaneous widgets

Back when the author of this modest work had fewer cares, he spent a lot of time
playing a game called Final Fantasy 7. In his opinion, it has to be one of the best
games ever made. Despite its grainy graphics[1], the story-line and game play are quite

---

[1]The 1997 version had grainy graphics. Final Fantasy 7 Rebirth Patch 1.020 which was released on 21st
March 2024 has silky smooth graphics.

captivating. In one of the stages, players are introduced to an imaginary creature called a *Chocobo*.

It looks like a cross between an ostrich and a chicken. Each one of them is unique and they're all adorable. Players can spend a lot of time at the in-game casino, gambling for credits to buy a better chocobo than the one they have. The biggest jackpot occurs when all 3 symbols align at 7, to give you "Lucky 7s". When said in Japanese, "All 7" becomes "Oru 7".

This subsection will teach you how to make a slot machine simulation using PyQt. Several new widgets are used to make it, so let's get an overview of each of them. The code contained in *widget6.py* simulates our slot machine.

5.7.1. QComboBox

A *QComboBox* provides a means of presenting a list of options to the user in a way that takes up the minimum amount of screen space. The reels of our simulator will be made using this widget. A combobox is a selection widget that displays the current item, and can pop up a list of selectable items. Comboboxes can contain pixmaps as well as strings, in our case we'll use numbers instead of images.

There are two signals emitted if the current item of a combobox changes, *currentIndexChanged()* and *activated()*. *currentIndexChanged()* is always emitted regardless of whether the change was done programmatically or by user interaction. *activated()* is only emitted when the change is caused by user interaction. The numerical symbols on our reels will be represented internally as strings. Each time a new combobox item is selected, a signal of type string will be sent to our signal handler.

QComboBox can use the model/view framework to populate its popup list. You can manually specify each of the items in a combobox object using the *addItem()* method, though this is tedious and prone to errors when you have a lot of data. In the sim, we use the *setModel()* to specify the model for the combobox. A *QStringListModel* object stores the list of items in our model.

The text of the currently selected item is accessed using the *currentText()* method.

5.7.2. QMovie

The *QMovie* class is a convenience class used to show simple animations without sound. You can instantiate a *QMovie* object by passing in the path to an animated image as its argument. To start the movie, call the *start()* method. QMovie will enter the running state, and emit *started()* and *stateChanged()*. To get the current state of the movie, call *state()*.

5.7.3. QLabel

This widget is used for displaying text or an image. No user interaction functionality is provided. You have already encountered it being used in Chapter 2 to display images. The movie class is overlaid on this widget so it can be displayed.

Tip

The *extend()* method appends elements to the end of a list. The resulting list contains all the elements of both lists.

For example:

```
a = [1, 2]
b = [3, "a", "b"]
a.extend(b)
```

When printed out, *a* contains

```
[1, 2, 3, 'a', 'b']
```

```
12 def initUI(self):
13   self.setWindowTitle('Slot machine sim')
14
15   myList = [] 1
16   myList.extend(range(0,10)) 2
17   myList = [str(i) for i in myList] 3
18
19   stringModel = QStringListModel(self) 4
20   stringModel.setStringList(myList) 5
21
22   self.comboBox1 = QComboBox(self) 6
23 ##        self.comboBox1.addItem("0") 7
24 ##        self.comboBox1.addItem("1")
25 ##        self.comboBox1.addItem("2")
```

```
26 ##          self.comboBox1.addItem("3")
27 ##          self.comboBox1.addItem("4")
28 ##          self.comboBox1.addItem("5")
29 ##          self.comboBox1.addItem("6")
30 ##          self.comboBox1.addItem("7")
31 ##          self.comboBox1.addItem("8")
32 ##          self.comboBox1.addItem("9")
```

1 **2** Manually writing out 0 to 9 is tiring. Plus, if your application requires a larger range, you're bound to make a mistake if you manually key in the integers. Python allows us to use the *range()* and *extend()* methods to elegantly populate our list.

3 This uses a list comprehension to convert each element of our list into a string. Our model expects a list containing values of type string.

4 **5** We declare the model that our comboboxes will use. We pass it the list we just created.

6 We declare an instance of our combobox widget.

7 As explained earlier, we can manually create combobox elements as shown here, or, we can do it intelligently using a model as shown in lines 33, 38 and 39.

*os.path.dirname(*file*)* **in line 46 finds and prepends the absolute path of the image source directory to the filename.**

```
46  self.movie =
QMovie(os.path.dirname(__file__)+"/"+"tenor.gif")
47
48  self.label1 = QLabel(self)
49  self.label1.move(50, 100)
50  self.label1.setGeometry(50, 100, 400, 500)
51  self.label1.setMovie(self.movie) 1
52
53  self.comboBox1.activated[int].connect(self.
onActivated) 2
54  self.comboBox2.activated[int].connect(self.
onActivated) 3
55  self.comboBox3.activated[int].connect(self.
onActivated)
56
```

```
57  self.resize(500, 650)
58  self.show()
59
60 @pyqtSlot(int)
61 def onActivated(self, text):
62  if(self.comboBox1.currentText() == '7' and
self.comboBox2.currentText() == '7'\
63     and self.comboBox3.currentText() == '7'):
64    self.movie.start() 4
65    #self.comboBox1.setEnabled(False)
66    print("Lotto!!!")
```

1   We use the *setMovie()* method of *QLabel* to connect the *QMovie* class to a widget.

2 **3** We connect the *activated()* signal from our comboxes to a slot. We pass a string containing the value of the current combobox item.

4   If the current value of all three comboboxes is 7, then we play our celebratory clip.

5.8. Summary

This chapter went over the most commonly used widgets in PyQt development.

Of course, more complex programs use a U.I. designer. The next chapter will introduce PyQt's visual design program.

5.9. References

- https://www.square-enix-games.com/en_US/ documents/notice-regarding-03-21-2024-update-final-fantasy-vii-rebirth
- https://doc.qt.io/qt-6/qwidget.html#size-prop
- https://doc.qt.io/qt-6/qwidget.html#adjustSize
- https://doc.qt.io/qt-6/qlineedit.html#textChanged
- https://doc.qt.io/qt-6/qlabel.html
- https://doc.qt.io/qt-6/qcalendarwidget.html#selectedDate-prop
- https://doc.qt.io/qt-6/qdate.html
- https://doc.qt.io/qt-6/qcheckbox.html#details
- https://doc.qt.io/qt-6/qcheckbox.html#stateChanged

- https://doc.qt.io/qt-6/qt.html#CheckState-enum
- https://doc.qt.io/qt-6/qlcdnumber.html#details
- https://doc.qt.io/qt-6/qslider.html#details
- https://en.wikipedia.org/wiki/FM_broadcast_band
- https://doc.qt.io/qt-6/qprogressbar.html#details
- https://doc.qt.io/qt-6/qtimeline.html#details
- https://doc.qt.io/qt-6/qtimeline.html#frameChanged
- https://doc.qt.io/qt-6/qopenglwidget.html#details
- http://www.not-enough.org/abe/manual/api-aa09/pyqt1.html
- https://en.wikipedia.org/wiki/Chocobo
- https://en.wikipedia.org/wiki/Slot_machine
- https://doc.qt.io/qt-6/qcombobox.html
- https://doc.qt.io/qt-6/qstringlistmodel.html

Chapter 6. FileLister

6.1. Qt Creator

For most large-scale projects you will need to use Qt Creator. This can be downloaded from:

https://github.com/qt-creator/qt-creator/releases

The professional version costs about $3950 per year(as of June 2024), but for our purposes, the free community version will work just as well. Download the community version program appropriate to your operating system.

After you set up Qt Creator, open it.

Tip

Full-size images of the following screenshots can be found in the *images* folder.

Figure 6.1. Qt Creator

Go to the File menu and create a new file.

Figure 6.2. New file window

Figure 6.3. Form template selection

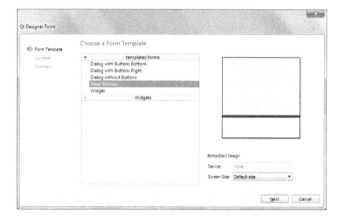

On the next screen, choose "Main Window" as shown.

Save the file in an appropriate location. After that you should get a new form that you can resize, "drag and drop" widgets on etc. Make yourself familiar with the interface, it's pretty simple.

We'll resize our main window a bit, since we don't need it to be that large. We'll also remove the automatically added menu and status bar since we don't plan on using them in this chapter.

All the form elements that your design has as well as their hierarchy, are listed (by default) on the right side of the Qt Creator window under "Object". You can easily remove objects by right clicking on them in that window. For now, we'll just resize our form and delete menu and status bar.

Figure 6.4. Make these adjustments

Once we do that, we're left with an (almost) empty form. The only object still left is *centralwidget* but we need it, so we won't change anything about it.
Now drag and drop from the "Widget Box" on the left-hand side a "List Widget" (not List View) widget and a "Push Button", drop them anywhere on the main form.

After resizing the window and its components everything looks perfect, right? Instead of using fixed positions and sizes of the elements in your application you should be using layouts. Fixed positions and sizes will look good on your end (at least until you resize the window), but you can never be sure that they'll look exactly the same on other machines and/or operating systems.

The main window already supports layouts, so we don't need to add any new ones to our form. Simply right click on the "Main Window" under the "Object" inspector and pick "Layout">"Lay out vertically".

Now the windows will scale correctly :)

Figure 6.5. Pick a layout

We've nailed the UI part down. The only thing left is to give the components mean-ingful names that we can access in our code. We could stick to the defaults, but, to avoid any confusion it's best to rename our components.

Change the button from its default name *pushButton* to *btnBrowse*. Also, change the "text" attribute of the button to *Pick a folder*!

Figure 6.6. Change attributes here

Save the file you've created. In my case, I named the file *mainwindow.ui*
This ".ui" file contains an XML representation of the widgets and properties in their design. For those familiar with Android development, this is like a layout XML file. To convert it into its Python equivalent we use the pyuic6 component. This component

was installed along with PyQt. Once you locate it on your system, run the following command:

pyuic6 mainwindow.ui -o mainwindow.py

 Tip

Still can't find pyuic? Run the following:

```
pip install pyqt6-tools
```

You should now have a file called *mainwindow.py*. This is a computer generated file and it's best not to edit it. Let's walk through the file named *fileLister.py*.

```
5 from mainwindow import Ui_MainWindow 1
```

1   We'll also need the file we just generated. Please note that Python is case sensitive! If you change the name from *mainwindow* to *mainWindow*, the interpreter will flag you.

The code is structured as a single class that is derived from the Python object type. The name of the class is the name of the top level object set in Creator with Ui_ prepended. (In the C++ version, the class is defined in the Ui namespace.) We refer to this class as the form class.

The class contains a method called *setupUi()*. This takes a single argument which is the widget in which the user interface is created. The type of this argument (typically *QDialog*, *QWidget* or *QMainWindow*) is set in Creator. We refer to this type as the Qt base class. Since the design file will be completely overwritten each time we change something in the design and recreate it, we will not be writing any code in it. Instead, we'll create a new class ie *ExampleApp* that we'll combine with the design code so that we can use all of its features.

```
10          self.setupUi(self)  # This is defined in the
file automatically generated, mainwindow.py
11                              # It sets up layout and
widgets defined there
12          self.btnBrowse.clicked.connect(self.
browse_folder) 1
13          self.show()
14
```

```
15      def browse_folder(self):
16          self.listWidget.clear() # In case there are
any existing elements in the list 2
17          directory =
QFileDialog.getExistingDirectory(self, 3
18

    "Pick a folder")
19              # execute getExistingDirectory dialog and
set the directory variable to be equal
20              # to the user selected directory
21

22          if directory: # if user didn't pick a
directory don't continue 4
23              for file_name in
os.listdir(directory): # for all files, if any, in the
directory 5
24                  self.listWidget.addItem(file_name)
 # add file to the listWidget 6
```

[1]   All of the following code is written inside the *ExampleApp* class. Let's start with the *Pick a folder* button. Just like in the previous chapter, we use this line to connect a button event, such as a mouse click, to a function. And add it to the *__init__* method of our *ExampleApp* class, so that it's set up when the application starts.

btnBrowse is the name of the button object we defined in Qt Creator.

[2] [3] To get the directory browser dialog we can use the built in *QtGui.QFileDialog.getExistingDirectory*.

[4]   If the user picks a directory, the *directory* variable will be equal to the absolute path of the selected directory, otherwise it's set to *None*.

[5]   This loops through the directory path. For each file found, its name is given to us in the *file_name* variable.

[6]   To add items to the listWidget we use *addItem()* method on it, and to clear all existing items simply use *self.listWidget.clear()*

Figure 6.7. FileLister output

A file browser dialog will open and the files in the chosen folder will be listed.

6.2. Summary

This chapter introduced you to designing apps using Qt Creator. Now it's time to shift gears to something even more complex.

This page inten-
tionally left blank

Chapter 7. Currency Exchange Rates App

We will build an app that connects to a web service, gets the exchange rate for some currencies, and then displays that data in a PyQt interface. We will use the currency-layer API(Application programming interface) to do this. Go to:

https://currencylayer.com/signup?plan=1

and sign up for a free account. Then log in, switch to the API tab and retrieve your API key. You will need it soon.

7.1. Designing the UI

If a picture is worth a thousand words, then a video is worth many more. Watch the video at

https://vimeo.com/261681292

The design of the UI is shown here.

Convert the UI design code into executable python code with the following command:
pyuic6 -o MainWindow.py -x mainwindow.ui

You already know what the *-o* switch does. The *-x* creates a script you can run right away without any further modification.

7.2. Switching back to Python

7.2.1. Web service communication

In the author's humble opinion, the python *requests* module is one of the easiest socket libraries he's ever used. Even with no past experience, you can get up and running with it in less than five minutes. Let's create a small script that will fetch the latest exchange rates from our web service. Do you have the API key from currencylayer handy? Let's use it here.

A screenshot of an interactive Python session the author had is shown below:

Tip

A full-size image of the following screenshot can be found in the *images* folder.

Figure 7.1. Working with the requests module

```
Python 3.10.6 (main, Aug 02 2022, 17:22:31) [GCC] on linux
Type "help", "copyright", "credits" or "license" for more information.
>>>
>>> import requests
>>>
>>> r = requests.get("https://api.apilayer.com/currency_data/live?source=USD&currencies=AUD%2CCAD%2CXAU%2CBTC", headers={"apikey":
 ]})
>>>
>>> r
<Response [200]>
>>>
>>> r.text
'{\n   "success": true,\n   "timestamp": 1661763304,\n   "source": "USD",\n   "quotes": {\n      "USDAUD": 1.459805,\n      "U
SDCAD": 1.307275,\n      "USDXAU": 0.000581,\n      "USDBTC": 5.0441799e-05\n   }\n}\n'
>>>
>>> r.json()
{'success': True, 'timestamp': 1661763304, 'source': 'USD', 'quotes': {'USDAUD': 1.459805, 'USDCAD': 1.307275, 'USDXAU': 0.000581, 'US
DBTC': 5.0441799e-05}}
>>>
>>> type(r.json())
<class 'dict'>
>>>
>>> b = r.json()
>>> b['timestamp']
1661763304
>>>
>>> b['quotes']
{'USDAUD': 1.459805, 'USDCAD': 1.307275, 'USDXAU': 0.000581, 'USDBTC': 5.0441799e-05}
>>>
```

The reader is encouraged to open an interactive session on their computer and try it for themselves. At the very least, open an interactive session and type in the first line: *import requests*

If you don't have the *requests* module installed on your system, you'll get an error message. You can then install the library on your system. The author created a mockup of his session and saved it as *servicecomm.py*. All you need to do is put in your API key to run it.

```
1 import requests
2
3 CURRENCYLAYER_API_KEY = "put your API key here"
4
5 #PS: The request URL may have changed by the time
you read this. Check the apilayer page to make sure
you're using the latest format!
6 r = requests.get("https://api.apilayer.com/
currency_data/live?source=USD&currencies=AUD%2CCAD%2CXAU
%2CBTC", headers={"apikey":CURRENCYLAYER_API_KEY}) 1

7
8 response = r.json() 2
```

```
 9
10 print("%.10f" % response['quotes']['USDBTC']) 3
```

1   A GET request is made to the web service. We pass in as parameters the cur-
    rencies whose exchange rates we want. The result of our request is stored in a
    variable named *r*.

2   The web service response is in JSON(JavaScript Object Notation) format. *r.j-
    son()* takes this response and converts it into a Python dictionary.

3   We parse our dictionary and print out the rate for the USDBTC pair. The *%.10f*
    takes a number in scientific form e.g., *4.9072449e-05*, removes the exponent
    i.e, *e-05*, and shifts the decimal point ten places to the left returning a number
    like *0.0000490786*.

Tip

A dictionary is a collection which is unordered, changeable and indexed.
In Python, dictionaries are written with curly brackets and they have
keys and values.

Create and print a dictionary:

```
thisdict = {
  "brand": "Ford",
  "model": "Mustang",
  "year": 1964
}
```

```
>>> print(thisdict)
{'brand': 'Ford', 'model': 'Mustang' , 'year'
 : 1964}
```

Get the value of the "model" key:

```
>>> x = thisdict["model"]
>>>
>>> print(x)
Mustang
```

If we combine this with the UI code from earlier, we'll have a fully functional script.

7.3. Putting it all together

You understand the UI code and understand how we communicate with the web service. Now let's put all the code together. The listing for *converter.py* is shown below.

```
16      def talkToService(self):
17          r = requests.get("https://api.apilayer.com/
currency_data/live?source=USD&currencies=AUD%2CCAD%2CXAU
%2CBTC",  headers={"apikey":CURRENCYLAYER_API_KEY})
18
19          response = r.json()
20
21          if r.status_code == 200: 1
22
self.cadLabel.setText(str(response['quotes']
['USDCAD']))
23
self.audLabel.setText(str(response['quotes']
['USDAUD']))
24
self.xauLabel.setText(str(response['quotes']
['USDXAU']))
25              self.btcLabel.setText("%.10f" %
response['quotes']['USDBTC'])
26          else: 2
27              print(response)
28              QtWidgets.QMessageBox.
critical(self, "Exception" ,
29                              "Something went
wrong!")
```

1   In an ideal situation only the code in the block(lines 21-25) runs. The *setText* method of the *QLabel* component allows us to set the text of our labels.

2   In case anything goes wrong for example: no Internet connection, no API key, or anything else unforeseen, the web service returns a status code other than 200.

Tip

Have a look at the code on line 22 inside the brackets.

str(response['quotes']['USDCAD'])

This illustrates type-casting. The *setText* method expects a variable of type string, yet *response['quotes']['USDCAD']* returns a floating point real number. To convert a real number into a string we wrap it inside a *str()* function.

Tip

Lambdas are one line functions. They are also known as anonymous functions in some languages. You use lambdas when you don't want to call a function twice in a program. They are just like normal functions and even behave like them.

The general form of a lambda function is:

```
lambda argument: manipulate(argument)
```

For example:

```
>>> add = lambda x, y: x + y
>>>
>>> print(add(1, 9))
10
>>>
```

Figure 7.2. The result of a successful execution

7.4. Summary

This chapter showed you how to add web functionality to your apps. If you understand the interaction your target(e.g. a web service) expects, you can quickly set up a demo or even a working app for your clients.

7.5. References

- https://doc.qt.io/qt-6/qmessagebox.html
- https://doc.qt.io/qt-6/qlabel.html#text-prop
- http://docs.python-requests.org/en/master/user/quickstart/
- https://doc.qt.io/qt-6/qlabel.html
- https://www.w3schools.com/python/python_dictionaries.asp

Chapter 8. PyQt databases and CSS styling

So far we've used the QT widgets just as they were shipped from the Qt Company. However, it's possible to customize their look and feel. But, before we begin we'll cover the basics of databases.

8.1. Qt Databases

It's assumed that you have a basic understanding of relational databases and SQL commands. PyQt is capable of interfacing with several types of databases including: MySQL, PostgreSQL, SQLite and ODBC. For the sake of uniformity across different platforms, we will work with SQLite in this chapter. For those who don't have a preferred SQLite browser, check out:

https://sqlitebrowser.org/

The database we will use is in this chapter's folder and is called *pyqt101.db*.

8.1.1. Connecting to the database and querying it

The code below is contained in a file named *connection-test.py*.

```
 4 def createConnection():
 5     filename =
os.path.join(os.path.dirname(__file__), "pyqt101.db")
 6
 7     db = QSqlDatabase.addDatabase('QSQLITE')  ❶
 8     db.setDatabaseName(filename)  ❷
 9
10     if not db.open():  ❸
11         QMessageBox.critical(None, "Cannot open
database",  ❹
12             "Unable to establish a database
connection.\n",
```

```
13                        QMessageBox.Cancel)
14            return False 5
15
16      query = QSqlQuery()
17
18      result = query.exec("SELECT Name FROM
`authors`") 6
19
20      while query.next():
21            print(query.value(0)) 7
22            #print(query.value("Name"))
23
24      db.close() 8
```

1   The *QSqlDatabase* class handles a connection to a database. An instance of *QSqlDatabase* represents the connection. The connection provides access to the database via one of the supported database drivers, which are derived from *QSqlDriver*. Create a connection by calling one of the static *addDatabase()* functions, where you specify the driver or type of driver to use (depending on the type of database) and a connection name.

2   Once the *QSqlDatabase* object has been created, set the connection parameters with *setDatabaseName()*, *setUserName()*, *setPassword()*, *setHostName()*, *set-Port()*, and *setConnectOptions()*. Then call *open()* to activate the physical connection to the database. The connection is not usable until you open it. Some of the connection parameters listed are optional. We only specify the database name parameter in this instance.

3 **4** We must anticipate problems while opening the database and allow our script
5   to exit gracefully.

6   The *QSqlQuery* class provides a means of executing and manipulating SQL statements. This class can be used to execute DML(data manipulation language) statements, such as SELECT, INSERT, UPDATE and DELETE, as well as DDL(data definition language) statements, such as CREATE TABLE. Successfully executed SQL statements set the query's state to active so that *isActive()* returns true. Otherwise, the query's state is set to inactive. You can loop through your results by checking whether the active state is true or not. Most times you can use the *exec(<put your SQL query here>)*

method to execute your queries as shown in line 18 of the code. It returns true if the query was successful. Otherwise, if you need to use parameters in your queries use the

prepare(<put your SQL query here>)

method.

7 Navigating records is performed with the following functions:

- *next()*
- *previous()*
- *first()*
- *last()*
- *seek()*

These functions allow you to move forward, backward or arbitrarily through the records returned by the query. If you only need to move forward through the results (e.g., by using *next()*), you can use *setForwardOnly()*, which will save a significant amount of memory overhead and improve performance on some databases. Once an active query is positioned on a valid record, data can be retrieved using *value()* as shown in line 21 of the code.

The *value()* function can take a numerical index or a string as a parameter, although the string variant is considered less efficient.

8 It's always a good habit to *close()* your database connection and free any acquired resources.

8.2. Models

Often the data from a database is displayed using PyQt components like lists or tables. PyQt provides two classes that extract data directly from the database:

1. *QsqlQueryModel*
2. *QsqlTableModel*

We examine QsqlQueryModel first, since it's easier to understand.

8.2.1. QsqlQueryModel

The *QSqlQueryModel* class provides a read-only data model for SQL result sets. You can read database entries, but you can't create, update or delete them. This class has a number of functions all of which can be looked up at:

https://doc.qt.io/Qt-6/qsqlquerymodel.html

We'll cover the more pertinent ones which are used in *model0.py*. An excerpt from this file is shown below.

```
19 ifnot db.open():
20   QMessageBox.critical(None, "Cannot open database",
21    "Unable to establish a database connection.\n",
22    QMessageBox.Cancel)
23   return False
24
25 sqm = QSqlQueryModel(parent = self)
26 sqm.setQuery("SELECT * FROM `authors`") 1
27
28 sqm.setHeaderData(1,
QtCore.Qt.Orientation.Horizontal, 'Author names') 2
29
30 self.setModel(sqm) 3
31 self.hideColumn(0) 4
32 self.resizeColumnsToContents() 5
33 self.horizontalHeader().
setSectionResizeMode(QHeaderView. ResizeMode.
Stretch) 6
34 self.verticalHeader().
setSectionResizeMode(QHeaderView. ResizeMode.
Stretch) 7
35 db.close()
```

1 *setQuery(<sql query here>, <optional parameter to specify database to be queried>)*

This is where you input your SQL query. If no database is specified, then the default connection will be used.

2   *setHeaderData(<int index>, <QtCore.Qt.Orientation i.e. Horizontal or Vertical>, <string value>, <role>)*

Have a look at line 5! Our class i.e. *MainWindow* is an instance of *QTableView*, so what we do on line 27 will be shown in a table. The *index* parameter specifies the index of the value we want to display from our query results. *Orientation* specifies whether our header will be horizontal or vertical. *Value* specifies the header name.

3   *QTableView* implements a table view that displays items from a model. We specify the model it should use to display its data on line 29. By default, all the data contained in the authors table, that is the author name and author id would be displayed.

4   Line 30 hides the author id column, so only author names are displayed.

5   Resize the width of the column to fit its contents. Comment this line out and note the difference!

6   Make the *QTableView* component occupy all the free space on the horizontal axis.

7   Make the *QTableView* component occupy all the free space on the vertical axis. Model–view–controller(MVC) is an architectural pattern commonly used for developing user interfaces that divides an application into three interconnected parts. This is done to separate internal representations of information from the way information is presented to and accepted from the user. The MVC design pattern decouples these major components allowing for efficient code reuse and parallel development.

Have a look at the image below!

The model communicates with a source of data, providing an interface for the other components in the architecture. The nature of the communication depends on the type of data source, and the way the model is implemented.

The view obtains model indexes from the model; these are references to items of data. By supplying model indexes to the model, the view can retrieve items of data from the data source.

In standard views, a delegate renders the items of data. When an item is edited, the delegate communicates with the model directly using model indexes

Figure 8.1. Image courtesy of qt.io

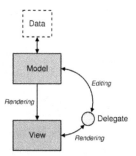

If the view and the controller objects are combined, the result is the model-view architecture. This still separates the way that data is stored from the way that it is presented to the user, but provides a simpler framework based on the same principles. This separation makes it possible to display the same data in several views, and to implement new types of views, without changing the underlying data structures. To allow flexible handling of user input, we introduce the concept of the delegate. The advantage of having a delegate in this framework is that it allows the way items of data are rendered and edited to be customized.

Those who would like to further acquaint themselves with MVC may look up the following resources:

https://doc.qt.io/qt-6/model-view-programming.html

https://en.wikipedia.org/wiki/Model–view–controller

8.2.2. QsqlTableModel

It's fun navigating through databases in read-only mode, but it quickly becomes boring. In order to perform CRUD(Create, Read, Update, Delete) operations on a database you need to use the *QsqlTableModel* class. This class provides an editable data model for a single database table. An exhaustive list of its functions can be found at:

https://doc.qt.io/qt-6/qsqltablemodel.html

The most common ones shall be explained using an example script. The code for the listing below can be found in *model1.py* in this chapter's folder.

```
5 def initializeModel(model):
6     model.setTable('authors1') ❶
```

```
 7      model.EditStrategy.OnFieldChange 2
 8      model.select() 3
 9      model.setHeaderData(1,
QtCore.Qt.Orientation.Horizontal, 'Author name(s)')
10
11 def createView(model):
12     view = QTableView()
13     view.setModel(model)
14     view.hideColumn(0)
15     #view.resizeColumnsToContents()
16     view.horizontalHeader().
setSectionResizeMode(QHeaderView.ResizeMode.Stretch)
17     view.verticalHeader().
setSectionResizeMode(QHeaderView.ResizeMode.Stretch)
18     return view
19
20 def addRecord():
21     # We insert an empty record into which the user
can enter their data
22     sqm.insertRow(sqm.rowCount()) 4
23
24 def delRecord() :
25     sqm.removeRow(view1.currentIndex().row()) 5
26     # We reload the data in the model, to remove an
empty "garbage" record
27     sqm.select() 6
```

1   An extra copy of the authors table has been provided for you to experiment with.

2   We pass an enumerated type to the edit strategy on line 7. Other possible values and their meanings are shown below.

Constant	Value	Description
QsqlTableModel.On-FieldChange	0	All changes to the model will be applied immediately to the database.
QsqlTableModel.On-RowChange	1	Changes to a row will be applied when the user selects a different row.
QsqlTableModel.On-ManualSubmit	2	All changes will be cached in the model until either submitAll() or revertAll() is called.

As soon as we make any changes to any row in our table, the values are immediately written to the database. In more complex systems you may want to store all your changes in a cache, then write them all at once. But for simple scripts like this, we've chosen to write all row changes as soon as they're made.

3 **6** The *select()* function in lines 8 and 27 refreshes the data in the model. On line 27, after deleting a selected row, the model is reloaded to remove the empty row in the database. In an ideal situation, you should be able to completely separate the user interface and data management code. But, the interaction between *delRecord()* and the UI breaks this flow.

5 *view1.currentIndex()* on line 25 returns the model index of the current item. The *row()* appended to it returns the row this index refers to. When you first run this script as shown in Figure 7.2, the model index automatically points at the first row in our table view. When you click the delete button, the first row is automatically deleted. But if you subsequently click on delete without highlighting a row, nothing will be deleted.

4 If the database supports returning the size of a query, the number of rows of the current query is returned. Otherwise, *rowCount()* on line 21 returns the number of rows currently cached on the client.

```
insertRow(<position x>)
```

adds a row at the x+1 row of the model.

Figure 8.2. QsqlTableModel demo

Go ahead and run *model1.py*. To insert a new record, click the appropriate button. A new row will be added after the last row of the table. Double click on this row to edit it and press the Enter key on your keyboard after you've finished. To delete a row, first highlight it with your mouse and click on the delete button.

8.2.3. QsqlRelationalTableModel

All our work with databases so far has involved working with a single table. But, the real power of databases comes from aggregating various tables together and presenting an interface to manipulate these components as one.

The *QSqlRelationalTableModel* class inherits all its methods from the *QSqlTableModel* class and, in addition to them, defines the following methods that you may find useful:

1. *setRelation(<specify column index>, <QsqlRelation relation>)*: Lets the specified *column* be a foreign index specified by *relation*.
2. *setJoinMode(<Binding mode>)*: Specifies the *binding mode* for the entire model. We pass an enumerated type here. Its possible values and their meanings are shown below:

Constant	Value	Description
QSqlRelationalTable-Model.InnerJoin	0	Inner join mode, return rows when there is at least one match in both tables.
QSqlRelationalTable-Model.LeftJoin	1	Left join mode, returns all rows from the left table (table_name1), even if there are no matches in the right table (table_name2).

Let's examine the code for *model2.py*.

```
 5 def initializeModel(model):
 6       model.setTable('booksauthors')
 7       model.EditStrategy.OnManualSubmit
 8       model.dataChanged.connect(model.submitAll)
 9       model.setRelation(0,
QSqlRelation("authors", "id", "name")) 1
10       model.setRelation(1,
QSqlRelation("books", "id", "title"))2
11       model.setHeaderData(0,
QtCore.Qt.Orientation.Horizontal, 'Author name(s)')
12       model.setHeaderData(1,
QtCore.Qt.Orientation.Horizontal, 'Book title')
13       model.select()
```

1   The table view uses the model from the *booksauthors* table. If you run it now with both lines 9 and 10 commented out you get output similar to that shown in Figure 7.3. This simply reads the table and outputs its contents.

When the interpreter encounters
"authors", "id", "name"

on line 9, it takes the first column shown in Figure 7.3, then for every integer value x, it goes into the *authors* table and looks up the row whose *authorid* has a value of x. Then, from that row, it returns the corresponding value of the *name* column. For example, the first row in the *booksauthors* table has an *authorid* value of 1. PyQt takes this value of 1 and looks into the *authors* table to find the row whose *id* column also has a value of 1. Then from that row, it reads the value of the name column, which in this case is *William Shakespeare*.

❷ This line does something similar for the books table to give you what you see in Figure 7.5.

Figure 8.3. Lines 9-12 commented out

Figure 8.4. Line 10 commented out

Figure 8.5. Lines 9 and 10 both included. Lines 11 and 12 commented out

8.2.4. QSqlRelationalDelegate

The buttons in lines 62 and 63 of *model2.py* were commented out because changes made to the model aren't saved to the database. The *QSqlRelationalDelegate* class provides a delegate that is used to display and edit data from a *QsqlRelationalTable-Model*. It provides a combobox for fields that are foreign keys into other tables.

Figure 8.6. Using the QSqlRelationalDelegate class

For the sake of pedagogy, we will use a simpler data model than before. In *pyqt101.db* there are two tables: *drinks* and *category*. *Drinks* contains a list of well-known drinks like Fanta, Johnny Walker etc. We classify these into two different categories: alcoholic or non-alcoholic. The categories table contains these 2 categories. Have a look at *model3.py*. Most of it should be familiar to you based on what we've previously covered.

```
 5 def initializeModel(model):
 6     model.setTable('drinks')
 7     model.EditStrategy.OnRowChange 1
 8     model.setHeaderData(1,
QtCore.Qt.Orientation.Horizontal, 'Name')
 9     model.setHeaderData(2,
QtCore.Qt.Orientation.Horizontal, 'Type of drink')
10     model.setRelation(2,
QSqlRelation('category', 'id', 'drinktype'))
11     model.select()
12
13 def createView(model):
14     view = QTableView()
15     view.setModel(model)
16     view.setItemDelegate(QSqlRelationalDelegate
(view)) 2
17     view.hideColumn(0)
18     view.horizontalHeader().
setSectionResizeMode(QHeaderView.ResizeMode.Stretch)
19     view.verticalHeader().
setSectionResizeMode(QHeaderView.ResizeMode.Stretch)
20     return view
21
22 def addRecord():
23     model.insertRow(model.rowCount())
24     view.scrollToBottom() 3
25
26 def delRecord():
```

```
27       model.deleteRowFromTable(view.currentIndex().
row()) 4
28       model.select()
```

1   The first difference is on this line. We write to our database any time that changes to a row in our model are made.

2   Unlike our previous example, we set the item delegate for the whole view as shown here.

3   This line automatically scrolls down to the last row of our view.

4   The most drastic departure from our previous script is on this line. Earlier on we'd used the *removeRow()* method. However, when used in this manner, changes are only made to the model and aren't written to the database. If we want to commit our changes to the database, we must use *deleteRowFromTable()*.

Have you run the script yet? The view is a bit quirky. When you add a new row, be sure to press Enter on your keyboard after you enter in all the required data. When the asterisk in the leftmost column changes and becomes a number, then you can rest assured that the data has been written to the database.

8.3. CSS Styling

Style sheets in Qt are based on the CSS2 specification which can be found at: https://www.w3.org/TR/2011/REC-CSS2-20110607/#minitoc

We will cover the basic rules and then look at a pretty cool example.

8.3.1. Style Rules

In the style rule below, *QPushButton* is the selector and *{ color: red }* is the declaration. The rule specifies that *QPushButton* and its subclasses should use red as their foreground text color.

Qt style sheets are generally case insensitive (i.e., *color, Color, COLOR,* and *cOloR* refer to the same property). The only exceptions are class names, object names, and Qt property names, which are case sensitive.

Several selectors can be specified for the same declaration, using commas (,) to separate the selectors. For example, the rule

```
QPushButton, QLineEdit, QComboBox { color: red }
```

is equivalent to this sequence of three rules:

```
QPushButton { color: red }
QLineEdit { color: red }
QComboBox { color: red }
```

The declaration part of a style rule is a list of < *property*: *value* > pairs, enclosed in braces and separated with semicolons. For example:

```
QPushButton { color: red; background-color: white }
```

A list of properties that you can manipulate can be found at:

https://doc.qt.io/Qt-6/stylesheet-reference.html#list-of-properties

8.3.2. Selector Types

All the examples so far have used the simplest type of selector- the Type Selector. Qt style sheets support all the selectors defined in CSS2. The table below summarizes the most useful types of selectors.

Selector	Example	Explanation
Universal Selector	*	Matches all widgets.
Type Selector	QPushButton	Matches instances of QPushButton and of its subclasses.
Property Selector	QPushButton[flat="false"]	Matches instances of QPushButton that are not flat. This selector may also be used to test dynamic properties. Instead of =, you can also use ~= to test whether a Qt property of type QStringList contains a given QString.
Class Selector	.QPushButton	Matches instances of QPushButton, but not of its subclasses. This is equivalent to *[class~="QPushButton"].
ID Selector	QPushButton#okButton	Matches all QPushButton instances whose object name is okButton.
Descendant Selector	QDialog QPushButton	Matches all instances of QPushButton that are descendants (children, grandchildren, etc.) of a QDialog.
Child Selector	QDialog > QPushButton	Matches all instances of QPushButton that are direct children of a QDialog.

8.3.3. Sub-Controls

For styling complex widgets, it is necessary to access subcontrols of the widget, such as the drop-down button of a *QComboBox* or the up and down arrows of a *QSpinBox*. Selectors may contain subcontrols that make it possible to restrict the application of a rule to specific widget subcontrols. For example:

```
QComboBox::drop-down { image: url(dropdown.png) }
```

The above rule styles the drop-down button of all QComboBoxes. Sub-controls are always positioned with respect to another element – a reference element. This reference element could be the widget or another sub-control. For example, the *::drop-down* of a *QComboBox* is placed, by default, in the top right corner of the Padding rectangle of the *QComboBox*.

A list of Stylable Widgets for the Sub-controls to use to style a widget and their default positions can be found at:

https://doc.qt.io/Qt-6/stylesheet-reference.html#list-of-stylable-widgets

A list of supported sub-controls can be found at:

https://doc.qt.io/Qt-6/stylesheet-reference.html#list-of-sub-controls

8.3.4. Pseudo-States

Selectors may contain pseudo-states that restrict the application of the rule based on the widget's state. Pseudo-states appear at the end of the selector, with a colon (:) in between. For example, the following rule applies when the mouse hovers over a *QPushButton*:

```
QPushButton:hover { color: white }
```

Pseudo-states can be negated using the exclamation operator. For example, the following rule applies when the mouse does not hover over a *QRadioButton*:

```
QRadioButton:!hover { color: red }
```

Pseudo-states can be chained, in which case a logical AND is implied. For example, the following rule applies to when the mouse hovers over a checked *QCheckBox*:

```
QCheckBox:hover:checked { color: white }
```

Negated pseudo-states may appear in pseudo-state chains. For example, the following rule applies when the mouse hovers over a *QPushButton* that is not pressed:

```
QPushButton:hover:!pressed { color: blue; }
```

If needed, logical OR can be expressed using the comma operator:

```
QCheckBox:hover, QCheckBox:checked { color: white }
```

Pseudo-states can appear in combination with subcontrols. For example:

```
QComboBox::drop-down:hover { image:
  url(dropdown_bright.png) }
```

A complete list of pseudo-states provided by Qt widgets can be found at:
https://doc.qt.io/Qt-6/stylesheet-reference.html#list-of-pseudo-states

8.3.5. Conflict Resolution

Conflicts arise when several style rules specify the same properties with different values. Consider the following:

```
QPushButton#okButton { color: gray }
QPushButton { color: red }
```

Both rules match *QPushButton* instances called *okButton* and there is a conflict for the color property. To resolve this conflict, we must take into account the **specificity** of the selectors. In the above example, *QPushButton#okButton* is considered more specific than *QPushButton*, because it (usually) refers to a single object, not to all instances of a class.

Similarly, selectors with pseudo-states are more specific than ones that do not specify pseudo-states. Thus, the following style specifies that a *QPushButton* should have white text when the mouse is hovering over it, otherwise red text:

```
QPushButton:hover { color: white }
QPushButton { color: red }
```

Here's a tricky one:

```
QPushButton:hover { color: white }
QPushButton:enabled { color: red }
```

Here, both selectors have the same specificity, so if the mouse hovers over the button while it is enabled, the second rule takes precedence. If we want the text to be white in that case, we can reorder the rules like this:

```
QPushButton:enabled { color: red }
QPushButton:hover { color: white }
```

Alternatively, we can make the first rule more specific:

```
QPushButton:hover:enabled { color: white }
QPushButton:enabled { color: red }
```

For determining the specificity of a rule, Qt Style Sheets follow the CSS2 Specification which can be found at:

http://www.w3.org/TR/REC-CSS2/cascade.html#specificity

8.3.6. Cascading

Style sheets can be set on the *QApplication*, on parent widgets, and on child widgets. An arbitrary widget's effective style sheet is obtained by merging the style sheets set on the widget's ancestors (parent, grandparent, etc.), as well as any style sheet set on the *QApplication*.

When conflicts arise, the widget's own style sheet is always preferred to any inherited style sheet, irrespective of the specificity of the conflicting rules. Likewise, the parent widget's style sheet is preferred to the grandparent's, etc.

One consequence of this is that setting a style rule on a widget automatically gives it precedence over other rules specified in the ancestor widgets' style sheets or the *QApplication* style sheet. Consider the following example. First, we set a style sheet on the *QApplication*:

```
qApp->setStyleSheet("QPushButton { color: white }");
```

Then we set a style sheet on a *QPushButton* object:

```
myPushButton->setStyleSheet("* { color: blue }");
```

The style sheet on the *QPushButton* forces the *QPushButton* (and any child widget) to have blue text, in spite of the more specific rule set provided by the application-wide style sheet.

8.3.7. Inheritance

In classic CSS, when font and color of an item is not explicitly set, it gets automatically inherited from the parent. By default, when using Qt style sheets, a widget does **not** automatically inherit its font and color setting from its parent widget.

For example, consider a *QPushButton* inside a *QGroupBox*:

```
qApp->setStyleSheet("QGroupBox { color: red; } ");
```

The *QPushButton* does not have an explicit color set. Hence, instead of inheriting color of its parent *QGroupBox*, it has the system color. If we want to set the color on a *QGroupBox* and its children, we can write:

```
qApp->setStyleSheet("QGroupBox, QGroupBox * { color:
 red; }");
```

In contrast, setting a font and palette using *QWidget::setFont()* and *QWidget::setPalette()* propagates to child widgets.

If you would prefer that the font and palette propagate to child widgets, you can set the *Qt.AA_UseStyleSheetPropagationInWidgetStyles* flag, like this:

```
QCoreApplication.setAttribute(Qt.AA_UseStyleSheet
 PropagationInWidgetStyles, True)
```

When the widget-style font and palette propagation is enabled, font and palette changes made through Qt style sheets will behave as though the user had manually called the corresponding *QWidget.setPalette()* and *QWidget.setFont()* methods on all of the QWidgets targeted by the style sheet.

To help you understand this better have a look at *cssinheritance.py*.

```
58 if __name__ == '__main__':
59     app = QApplication(sys.argv)
60
61     app.setStyleSheet("QGroupBox { color: red; } ")
62
63     #app.setStyleSheet("QGroupBox, QGroupBox *
{ color: red; }")
64
65     #QCoreApplication.setAttribute\
66     #    (Qt.ApplicationAttribute.AA_UseStyleSheet
PropagationInWidgetStyles, True)
67     #app.setStyleSheet("QGroupBox { color: red; } ")
68
69     clock = Window()
```

First, run it as it is to see the default.

Figure 8.7. Default

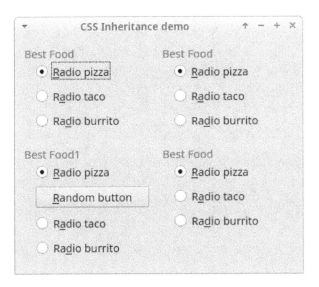

Comment out line 61 and un-comment line 63 to see the effect of "brute-forcing" inheritance.

Figure 8.8. Brute-forcing inheritance

This may have unforeseen consequences somewhere down the line. Comment out lines 61 and 63 and un-comment lines 65 and 66 to see the more elegant way of setting up inheritance.

Have a look at line 61 again! It illustrates one way to set styling one widget at a time, by calling the *setStyleSheet()* method on all your widgets. I will demonstrate how to set global CSS properties in the next section.

8.3.8. Example

Now for the demo that inspired the author to write this section on CSS. Drum-roll... He found this code online on a French website called *ilycode*. At the time of publishing, the article had been deleted.

Figure 8.9. Before applying CSS

In the chapter folder, run the script called *css-pre.py* to get something similar to what is shown above. The script presents the UI for a simple client registration page. Given what you already know about databases, you can create a back-end to process the registration details. Apart from lines 23-27, all the code in this script should be familiar to you. These lines set up a label. However, instead of putting text in the label, we load an image.

Run the script called *css-post.py* to see the effect of applying CSS styling to the UI.

Figure 8.10. After applying CSS

This script sets CSS properties on widget-by-widget basis. This is usually disadvantageous because you have to keep repeating things. For example, the text widgets on lines 33, 39, 45, 51, all repeat the following code:

```
setStyleSheet("background-color:#f7f7f7; color:#8e8e8e;
  padding-top: 5px; font-size:15px; padding-left:10px")
```

Apart from setting styling code locally, you can also set it up globally. Have a look at the code in *css-post-global.py*.

A variable is declared on line 11 that contains all the Style Sheet attributes for the script in one place. This Style Sheet is then applied on the QApplication instance as shown in line 37.

```
11          self.stylesheet = """
```

```
12
13          QPushButton{
14              background-color:#4e4e4e;
15              color:#ffffff;
16              font-size:15px;
17              border:1px solid #4e4e4e;
18          }
19
20          QMainWindow{
21              background-color:#ff9900;
22              /*background-color:#6e6e6e;*/
23          }
24
25          QTextEdit{
26              background-color:#44ff22;
27          }
28
29
30          """
31
32          self.initGUI()
33
34          self.window.setWindowTitle("With CSS
styling")
35          self.window.setGeometry(500, 100, 300,600)
36          self.window.show()
37          self.app.setStyleSheet(self.stylesheet)
38          sys.exit(self.app.exec())
```

If you want to override the style attributes for any widget, you can specify a widget-specific style sheet as shown on line 57.

```
56          self.email.setGeometry(25, 330,250,40)
57          self.email.setStyleSheet("background-
color:#f7f7f7; color:#8e8e8e; padding-top: 5px; font-
size:15px; padding-left:10px")
```

It's amazing how a few lines of code can dramatically enhance your app. The illustration below shows our app with line 57 of *css-post-global.py* commented out.

Figure 8.11. Eye candy

8.4. Summary

Many complex apps use databases to store some of their data. This chapter has introduced you to using databases in your apps. Although we've worked with SQLite databases, it's important to keep in mind that similar techniques will apply to MySQL or any other database supported by the PyQt framework.

CSS can help you soup up your UI. Use it whenever you can to draw your client's attention to specific parts of your interface and to make your apps look attractive.

8.5. References

- https://doc.qt.io/qt-6/qsqldatabase.html

- https://doc.qt.io/qt-6/qsqlquery.html
- https://doc.qt.io/Qt-6/qsqlquerymodel.html
- https://doc.qt.io/qt-6/qtableview.html
- https://doc.qt.io/qt-6/qsqltablemodel.html#EditStrategy-enum
- https://doc.qt.io/qt-6/qtsql-tablemodel-example.html
- https://doc.qt.io/qt-6/qabstractitemview.html#currentIndex
- https://doc.qt.io/qt-6/qmodelindex.html#row
- https://doc.qt.io/qt-6/qsqlrelationaltablemodel.html
- https://doc.qt.io/qt-6/qsqlrelationaldelegate.html
- https://doc.qt.io/qt-6/qsqlrelationaltablemodel.html#JoinMode-enum
- https://doc.qt.io/Qt-6/stylesheet-syntax.html
- https://doc.qt.io/qt-6/stylesheet-reference.html
- https://www.w3.org/TR/2011/REC-CSS2-20110607/#minitoc
- https://doc.qt.io/Qt-6/stylesheet-examples.html

This page inten-
tionally left blank

Chapter 9. Radio App

In this chapter we'll explore a radio app that uses PyQt6.

Important

For Windows users, you may refer to Appendix C for instructions on how to set up Docker, so that you may follow along.

For those following along on Unix-like systems other than Ubuntu, I trust that you'll be able to adapt the install instructions to suit your particular OS. Alternatively, if you have installed Docker, you may find it easier and more convenient to build a container that will run all the scripts below. Please refer to Appendix C if this is the case.

9.1. Setting up

You first need to set up a Python package called *gi*. Using the appropriate version of pip for Python3 install *gi* with the command:

pip install PyGObject

Important

Most people will encounter an error while installing *PyGObject*. Oftentimes this error will be caused by a missing system library. Please visit the following URL and follow the OS-specific instructions there to remedy this:

https://pygobject.readthedocs.io/en/latest/getting_started.html

This will install the *gi* package on your system if you didn't already have it. To ensure that it works, run the script titled *hello.py* in the source folder for this chapter.

If everything goes well your output should look similar to the following:

Figure 9.1. Is *gi* installed on your system?

You will also need version 1.x of Gstreamer. Linux users will find instructions at: https://gstreamer.freedesktop.org/documentation/installing/on-linux.html Windows, macOS, Android, and iOS users can find binaries at: https://gstreamer.freedesktop.org/download/

Now you're all set for the next part.

9.2. Gstreamer

Back when I was in grade school, classes on Friday used to end at 3:20 pm. I'd usually end up at my friend Mo's house. His dad was a mechanic and had all sorts of cool hardware that I liked going through while he was still at work. My folks had dull office jobs and their work things weren't worth going through.

One day we discovered an electronics puzzle kit among his dad's things. We could make simple circuits by snapping puzzle pieces together to match patterns shown in a book that accompanied the kit. I'd always loved radio and we followed the instructions to assemble a simple crystal radio. I was cynical about the claim that one could make a radio without any electricity and wasn't surprised when it didn't work. Mo read the instructions through again and we spent half an hour fiddling with a water tap before we got it to work.

It turned out that we'd assembled it correctly, but we hadn't grounded it. There was a faint signal on the earphones from a local AM station, but it worked. Each puzzle piece had an electric circuit component soldered underneath it as well as connectors on either side that joined to other circuit components. It was quite complex for 10-year-old kids without any electronics training, but the pictures on top of the puzzle pieces made it look and feel like a game. Search Google for "Snap Circuits". What we used was similar, but wasn't as colorful as today's models.

Gstreamer is similar to those snap circuits. It comes with various components, that you can assemble together to make many different multimedia tools like a DVD player, streaming Internet radio player and recorder etc. The team that won the 2016 Nobel Prize for Physics used a Gstreamer plugin to help them detect gravity waves. If you have a Samsung flat-screen TV or have watched a movie on an airplane, they were probably using Gstreamer.

I will not give a comprehensive tutorial on Gstreamer(consult their website for that, links in the references section), I only give you an overview that will allow you to follow the code for this chapter. If you're not technically-inclined, you can think of this like building a puzzle(like Mo and I did) and not worry too much about what's beneath the puzzle pieces you're assembling.

9.2.1. Pipeline

The substrate or puzzle board on which all puzzle pieces(elements) are mounted is called the pipeline. Elements process the data(for example output from your favorite Internet radio site) as it moves downstream from the source elements, to sink elements(like your speaker) passing through filter elements. Playing media straight from the Internet without storing it locally is known as streaming.

Figure 9.2. Image courtesy of gstreamer.freedesktop.org

9.2.2. Elements

The ports through which GStreamer elements communicate with each other are called pads. There exist sink pads, through which data enters an element, and source pads, through which data exits an element. It follows naturally that source elements only contain source pads, sink elements only contain sink pads, and filter elements contain both. Source pads produce data, sink pads consume data.

Figure 9.3. Data flows "down" the pipeline from left to right (image courtesy of gstreamer.freedesktop.org)

A demultiplexer for digital media files, or media demultiplexer also called a file split-ter by laymen or consumer software providers, is software that breaks down individ-ual elementary streams of a media file, e.g., audio, video, or subtitles and sends them to their respective decoders for actual decoding. A media file for example an mp4 file is a container that has several streams of data packed together. An mp4 player will be able to read and unpack these streams of audio, video and subtitles in a process called decoding, then present them to you in a coherent manner, directing output to your speakers and video screen.

Media demultiplexers are not decoders themselves, but are format container handlers that separate program streams from a file and supply them to their respective audio, video, or subtitles decoders. A demuxer contains one sink pad, through which the muxed data arrives, and multiple source pads, one for each stream found in the con-tainer.

A pipeline for a basic ogg player is illustrated below:

Figure 9.4. Image courtesy of gstreamer.freedesktop.org

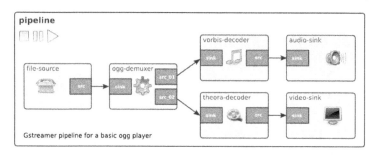

Ogg is an open source file format. To confirm that you have a working version of Gstreamer tools installed on your system, run the following command:

gst-launch-1.0 videotestsrc ! autovideosink

This will open a window with a video test pattern on your system. If the above command run successfully, try the following command:

gst-launch-1.0 audiotestsrc ! autoaudiosink

This will generate a 440 Hz audio test tone. Switch on your speakers to confirm that it works. Next we're going to combine the audio and video in one pipeline and output the result as an ogg file. Type in:

gst-launch-1.0 audiotestsrc ! vorbisenc ! oggmux name=mux ! filesink location=file.ogg videotestsrc ! theoraenc ! mux.

and let it run for at least 30 seconds.

You can terminate it by pressing *Ctrl+C*. This will output 30 seconds of data into a file called *file.ogg*. Inspect your current working directory and confirm that this file exists!

Most of the above command should be familiar to you. Specifying the *name* property of an element lets you use it more than once. We take the output of the audio test source, feed it into an ogg muxer and name it *mux*. We then use *mux* again, by feeding the output of a video test source into it. Finally, we take the combined result and direct it into a file named *file.ogg*.

Remember, muxing is packing several streams of data for example audio, video and subtitles into a single container file. In effect what we've done is take Figure 9.4 above and run it from right to left.

9.2.3. Pads

Pads are an element's interface to the outside world. Data streams from one element's source pad to another element's sink pad. In addition to direction of data flow, pads have another important property- availability.

A pad can have any of three availabilities: always, sometimes and on-request. The meaning of those three types is exactly as it says: always pads always exist, sometimes pad exist only in certain cases (and can disappear randomly), and on-request pads appear only if explicitly requested by applications. For this basic introduction, we will ignore request pads.

Some elements might not have all of their pads when the element is created. This can happen, for example, with an Ogg demuxer element. The element will read the Ogg stream and create dynamic pads for each contained elementary stream (vorbis, theora) when it detects such a stream in the Ogg stream. Likewise, it will delete the pad when the stream ends.

On your CLI run the following:
gst-inspect-1.0 oggdemux
and inspect the output.

The element has only one pad: a sink pad called "sink". The other pads are "dormant". You can see this in the pad template because there is an "Exists: Sometimes" property. Depending on the type of Ogg file you play, the pads will be created. We will see that this is very important when you are going to create dynamic pipelines. You can attach a signal handler to an element to inform you when the element has created a new pad from one of its "Sometimes" pad templates.

9.2.4. Element states

After being created, an element will not actually perform any actions yet. You need to change an elements' state to make it do something. GStreamer knows four element states, each with a very specific meaning. These four states are:

1. GST_STATE_NULL: this is the default state. No resources are allocated in this state, so, transitioning to it will free all resources. The element must be in this state when its reference count reaches 0 and it is freed.
2. GST_STATE_READY: in the ready state, an element has allocated all of its global resources, that is, resources that can be kept within streams. You can think about opening devices, allocating buffers and so on. However, the stream is not opened in this state, so the stream position is automatically zero. If a stream was previously opened, it should be closed in this state, and position, properties and such should be reset.
3. GST_STATE_PAUSED: in this state, an element has opened the stream, but is not actively processing it. An element is allowed to modify a stream's position, read and process data and such to prepare for playback as soon as state is changed to PLAYING, but it is not allowed to play the data which would make the clock run. In summary, PAUSED is the same as PLAYING but without a running clock. Elements going into the PAUSED state should prepare themselves for moving over to the PLAYING state as soon as possible. Video or audio outputs would, for example, wait for data to arrive and queue it so they can play it right after the state change. Also, video sinks can already play the first frame (since this does not affect

the clock yet). Autopluggers could use this same state transition to already plug together a pipeline. Most other elements, such as codecs or filters, do not need to explicitly do anything in this state, however.

4. GST_STATE_PLAYING: in the PLAYING state, an element does exactly the same as in the PAUSED state, except that the clock now runs.

You can change the state of an element using the function *set_state()*. If you set an element to another state, GStreamer will internally traverse all intermediate states. So if you set an element from NULL to PLAYING, GStreamer will internally set the element to READY and PAUSED in between.

9.2.5. Bringing it all together

Is your head spinning after that whirlwind tour of Gstreamer? It's time to bring it all together with a simple PyQt example that will reinforce what you've learnt so far. In the folder for this chapter open a file named *baby.py*. We will programmatically implement Figure 9.4 and you will get to see an example of dynamic pipelines in action.

Run the following command:
python3 baby.py

Click on the start button, this will open a file selection dialog. Select the ogg file we created in the previous section. It will automatically start playing. You can stop it by clicking "Stop" in the main window. For this simple player, only start and stop states are possible. The next section will explain how it works.

Figure 9.5. First screen of your player

Figure 9.6. Select the file you created in the last section

Figure 9.7. The file is automatically played

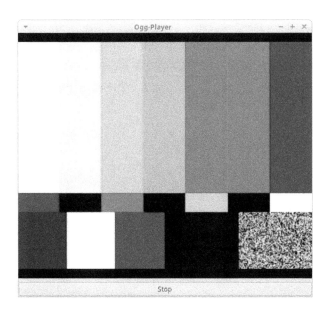

9.2.6. Explanation of the code

First we'll cover the UI setup.

Most Gstreamer scripts will have lines 2 to 5. They ensure that Gstreamer 1.x is installed on the system before the script runs.

```
1 import sys
2 import gi
3 gi.require_version('Gst', '1.0')
4 gi.require_version('GstVideo', '1.0')
5 from gi.repository import Gst, GstVideo
```

You've encountered a vertical box layout in a previous chapter. Lines 20 and 21 create an instance of one here and set it to occupy the entire area of the window. Its internal widgets will expand to occupy as much space as possible(which is why the button looks kind of stretched). We use a QWidget instance on line 22. We will redirect our videosink output into this widget.

```
14      def initUI(self):
```

```
15          self.setWindowTitle('Ogg-Player')
16          self.resize(546, 475)
17          self.setGeometry(0, 0, 546, 475)
18
19          self.verticalLayout = QVBoxLayout(self)
20          self.verticalLayout. setContentsMargins
(0, 0, 0, 0)
21
22          self.windowWidget = QWidget(self)
```

Now we look at the basic gstreamer setup flow.

Before you do anything, you must initialize Gstreamer. Line 34 is another line that most Gstreamer scripts have. Line 35 creates a pipeline. We then create file-source and demuxer elements. These will be linked together in our pipeline later.

```
33 def initPlayer(self):
34  Gst.init(None)
35  self.player = Gst.Pipeline.new("player")
36  source = Gst.ElementFactory.make("filesrc", "file-
source")
37  demuxer =
Gst.ElementFactory.make("oggdemux", "demuxer")
```

The elements on each path are created in lines 43-49. Did you notice the two extra elements that aren't in Figure 9.4? The script will probably run just fine without _audioconv_ and _videoconv_. According to the Gstreamer documentation, these extra elements are necessary to guarantee that the pipeline can be linked. The capabilities of the audio and video sinks depend on the hardware, and you do not know at design time if they will match the capabilities produced by the audio and video test sources. If the capabilities match, these elements act in "pass-through" mode and do not modify the signal, having negligible impact on performance.

```
38  demuxer.connect("pad-added",
self.demuxer_callback) ▮
39
```

```
40  self.queuea =
Gst.ElementFactory.make("queue", "queuea") 2
41  self.queuev =
Gst.ElementFactory.make("queue", "queuev") 3
42
43  self.audio_decoder =
Gst.ElementFactory.make("vorbisdec", "vorbis-decoder")
44  audioconv =
Gst.ElementFactory.make("audioconvert", "convertera")
45  audiosink =
Gst.ElementFactory.make("autoaudiosink", "audio-
output")
46
47  self.video_decoder =
Gst.ElementFactory.make("theoradec", "theora-decoder")
48  videoconv =
Gst.ElementFactory.make("videoconvert", "converterv")
49  videosink =
Gst.ElementFactory.make("autovideosink", "video-
output")
```

1 As mentioned earlier, a pad can have 3 capabilities. An oggdemux element has "sometimes" capabilities. Depending on the data fed into it, it will create dynamic pads for each stream it finds. Since we're using the file we created earlier, the *demuxer_callback()* function will be called twice for each stream contained in our file.

2 **3** Have a look at Figure 9.4 again! The output from the demuxer is directed down two separate paths, one for audio another for video. The audio output in our program will be represented by *self.queuea*, while the video will be represented using *self.queuev*.

After we've created all the elements of our pipeline, we bring them together as shown on lines 51-61.

```
51          self.player.add(source)
52          self.player.add(demuxer)
53          self.player.add(self.audio_decoder)
54          self.player.add(audioconv)
```

```
55          self.player.add(audiosink)
56          self.player.add(self.queuea)
57
58          self.player.add(self.video_decoder)
59          self.player.add(videoconv)
60          self.player.add(videosink)
61          self.player.add(self.queuev)
```

Lines 63-70 link the elements on each path together.

```
63   source.link(demuxer)
64   self.queuea.link(self.audio_decoder)
65   self.audio_decoder.link(audioconv)
66   audioconv.link(audiosink)
67
68   self.queuev.link(self.video_decoder)
69   self.video_decoder.link(videoconv)
70   videoconv.link(videosink)
71
72   bus = self.player.get_bus()  1
73   bus.add_signal_watch()  2
74   bus.connect('message', self.on_message)  3
75   bus.enable_sync_message_emission()  4
76   bus.connect("sync-message::element",
self.on_sync_message)  5
```

1 2 The pipeline transmits signals when it's in different states. For example, if we
3   come to the end of a playing file, a stop notification will be emitted. Or if there's
       an error, we can print out some debug information and gracefully exit.

4 5 This is for the video output. A "prepare-window-handle" message will be sent
       from the video sink. We set up a listener for this message and specify an action
       to take when we receive a message.

So far so good. The main obstacle we'll face is directing the output to the appropriate
devices. Gstreamer "needs" to know where to send the video output. Every *QWidget*
object has a window id property. We get this and pass it to Gstreamer.

**Please examine lines 79-90! We need to pick a file to pass to our file-source
element. We open a file selection dialog and filter it to only accept files with**

the ".ogg" extension. Once we find such a file, we change the pipeline to the
PLAYING state and change the button label to "Stop". The else case on line 88,
resets the pipeline if we stop a playing stream.

```
78 def start_stop(self):
79   if self.button.text() == 'Start':
80     filepath =
QFileDialog.getOpenFileName(self,"Choose a
file!", "","Ogg Files (*.ogg)")
81     #filepath returns a tuple containing ('/home/
yourpathhere/yourfilenamehere.ogg', 'Ogg Files (*.ogg)')
82     #we need to unpack this tuple to obtain a
filename we can use
83     #filepath[0] is a string containing the
filename we want for example /home/yourpathhere/
yourfilenamehere.ogg
84     if filepath:
85       self.button.setText('Stop')
86       self.player.get_by_name("file-
source").set_property("location", filepath[0])
87       self.player.set_state(Gst.State.PLAYING)
88   else:
89       self.player.set_state(Gst.State.NULL)
90       self.button.setText('Start')
```

Have a look back at lines 63 and 64. Did you notice we didn't link our demuxer to
our queue elements? The demuxer output depends on the input data presented
to it. Sometimes it may only have audio output, other times video or even text
output. When it has output, a new pad is created. The code that handles this is
shown on lines 92-102. Lines 93-95 query the output of a new pad. If it has either
output of type audio or video, we connect it to the appropriate queue for further
processing.

```
92     def demuxer_callback(self, demuxer, newpad):
93         res = Gst.Pad.get_current_caps(newpad)
94         structure = Gst.Caps.get_structure(res, 0)
95         result = Gst.Structure.get_name(structure)
```

```
96              if "audio" in result:
97                  print(result)
98                  adec_pad =
self.queuea.get_static_pad("sink")
99                  newpad.link(adec_pad)
100             if "video" in result:
101                 vdec_pad =
self.queuev.get_static_pad("sink")
102                 newpad.link(vdec_pad)
```

Signal handling code is usually the same on many Gstreamer projects. The code that does this is on lines 104-113. Events are all put on a queue. We listen for two events- EOS(End of Stream) and ERROR. In case of EOS, we set the player button text back to "Start", showing that it's ready to receive new input. Setting the pipeline to null, frees all resources consumed by it. When the ERROR event is fired, we print an error and prepare to receive more input. Lines 115-119 define the handler we set up on line 76. We direct output to our videosink, show it the window to use for its output and specify that it should maintain its aspect ratio.

```
104     def on_message(self, bus, message):
105         t = message.type
106         if t == Gst.MessageType.EOS:
107             self.player.set_state(Gst.State.NULL)
108             self.button.setText('Start')
109         elif t == Gst.MessageType.ERROR:
110             self.player.set_state(Gst.State.NULL)
111             err, debug = message.parse_error()
112             print('Error: %s' % err, debug)
113             self.button.setText('Start')
114
115     def on_sync_message(self, bus, message):
116         if message.get_structure().get_name()
== 'prepare-window-handle':
117             videosink = message.src
118             videosink.set_property("force-aspect-
ratio", True)
```

```
119
 videosink.set_window_handle(self.windowWidget.winId())
```

9.3. Radio app

We finally get to the radio app. This app incorporates Gstreamer to stream data from an Internet radio station. It has a beautiful UI that incorporates PyQt elements to provide a lot of the functionality you'd expect from a media-player and then some. In this section we'll only focus on the PyQt code. From the CLI run the following command: *python3 qt6radio.py*

If everything is set up correctly you should see output similar to the following:

Figure 9.8. Our radio app

Unlike many radio players, this one allows you to record what you listen to as an mp3 file. This time we'll focus on the UI part of the app.

After loading the icons, we set the default radio station from our database on line 45. Lines 50-54 demonstrate how to set button icons.

```
45 self.station=radio_db[0][0]
46 self.old_title=""
47
48 # Source for icons
49 # https://icons8.com/icon/set/media-player/all
50 self.app_icon=QIcon(icons_dir+"/audio-wave-64.png")
51 self.play_icon=QIcon(icons_dir+"/play-64.png")
52 self.stop_icon=QIcon(icons_dir+"/stop-64.png")
```

```
53 self.rec_icon=QIcon(icons_dir+"/downloads-64.png")
54 self.mute_icon=QIcon(icons_dir+"/mute-64.png")
```

Line 16 reads from a file containing a list of radio stations and stores the result in a variable named *radio_db*. Lines 74 to 76 populate our combobox with all the entries in our radio station database. On line 77 we set up an event handler which is called anytime we access the combobox. Even if we don't change the station, as long as we click on the combobox this event handler will be called.

```
71 def initUI(self):
72   label = QLabel("Radio station: ", self)
73
74   combo = QComboBox(self)
75   for i in radio_db:
76     combo.addItem(i[0])
77   combo.activated[int].connect(self.onActivated)
```

This is the event handler triggered when we access the combobox. If the radio is currently playing, it is stopped. The index of whichever item is selected on the combobox is looked up in our radio database and passed to our Gstreamer component, ready to be streamed. The log component in line 165, refers to the non-editable textbox you can see in Figure 9.8. We also change the main window title, every time we change stations.

```
151 def onActivated(self, idx):
152   # when changing station, do the following
153   # 1. stop playing old station
154   # 2. switch to new station
155   # 3. play new station
156
157   # 1. If playing, stop playing
158   self.stop()
159
160   # 2. Swtich to new station
161   #self.pipeline.set_state(Gst.State.NULL)
162   self.station=radio_db[idx][0]
163   self.setWindowTitle(radio_db[idx][0])
```

```
164  self.http_source.set_property("location",
 radio_db[idx][1])
165  self.log.appendPlainText("%s: Switch to station %s"
166          % (time.asctime(time.localtime()),
167          self.station))
```

We set up our play button. We pass a "1" or True to several of its attributes like *setDefault* and *setCheckable*. *SetDefault* is what makes it look darker than the others, like its just been pressed. *setCheckable* allows us to interact with it. Clicking on uncheckable buttons doesn't trigger any events. We then set its event handler and icon.

```
79 self.playBtn=QPushButton(self)
80 self.playBtn.setDefault(1)
81 self.playBtn.setCheckable(1)
82 self.playBtn.setIcon(self.play_icon)
83 self.playBtn.resize(self.playBtn.sizeHint())
84 self.playBtn.clicked.connect(self.onPlay)
```

Lines 172-173 link the play button to its event handler whose code is shown below. After toggling some variables, it sends a GST_STATE_PLAYING to our pipeline.

```
220 self.playBtn=QPushButton(self)
221 self.playBtn.setDefault(1)
222 self.playBtn.setCheckable(1)
223 self.playBtn.setIcon(self.play_icon)
224 self.playBtn.resize(self.playBtn.sizeHint())
225 self.playBtn.clicked.connect(self.onPlay)
```

Lines 175-176 link the stop button to its event handler whose code is shown below. Its event handler sends a GST_STATE_NULL message to our pipeline. This stops anything that's playing and frees internal resources.

```
227 def stop(self):
228  self.playing=0
229  self.playBtn.setChecked(0)
230  self.stopBtn.setChecked(1)
```

```
231   self.pipeline.set_state(Gst.State.NULL)
232   self.mainloop.quit()
```

Lines 92-96 link the record button to its event handler whose code is shown below. The event handler checks to see if its already recording. If it is, it stops. If it's not recording and a stream is playing, it begins the recording process. If it's not recording and a stream isn't playing an error message is produced.

```
178 def onRec(self):
179   if self.recording:
180     self.log.appendPlainText("%s: Recording stop"
181           % (time.asctime(time.localtime())))
182     self.filesink.set_state(Gst.State.NULL)
183     self.filesink.set_property("location", "/dev/
null")
184     self.filesink.set_state(Gst.State.PLAYING)
185     self.recording=0
186   else:
187     if self.playing:
188       now=time.strftime("%y%m%d_%H%M%S")
189       self.log.appendPlainText("%s: Recording started"
190             % time.asctime(time.localtime()))
191       self.filesink.set_state(Gst.State.NULL)
192       self.filesink.set_property("location", "%s_
%s.mp3" %
193                   (now, self.station))
194       self.filesink.set_state(Gst.State.PLAYING)
195       self.recording=1
196     else:
197       self.log.appendPlainText("Recording not started.
" +
198             "No playing stream")
199     self.recBtn.setChecked(0)
```

Lines 102-106 link the mute button to its event handler whose code is shown below. In order to mute all we need to do is set the mute property of the audio sink.

```
201 def onMute(self):
202  if self.muteBtn.isChecked():
203    self.play_audio.set_property("mute", 1)
204  else :
205    self.play_audio.set_property("mute", 0)
```

Lines 108-111 link the volume slider to its event handler whose code is shown below. Its event handler sends the audio sink an appropriate signal depending on the current state as well as user input.

```
207 def onVolChanged(self, event):
208  pos=self.volCtrl.sliderPosition()
209  self.play_audio.set_property("volume",
 self.volMultiple*pos/100.0)
210  #print(self.play_audio.get_property("volume"))
211  if pos==0:
212    self.muteBtn.setChecked(1)
213    self.play_audio.set_property("mute", 1)
214  else:
215    self.muteBtn.setChecked(0)
216    self.play_audio.set_property("mute", 0)
217  #if self.volCtrl.event(QEvent.MouseButtonPress):
218  QToolTip.showText(QCursor.pos(), "%d" % pos, self)
```

The code below sets up the log window.

```
 98 self.log=QPlainTextEdit()
 99 self.log.setReadOnly(1)
100 self.log.setWordWrapMode(QTextOption.WrapMode.
 WordWrap) # No text wrap
```

9.4. Summary

Aren't you glad you took the time to understand a bit about how Gstreamer works? Your basic knowledge combined with what you already know about PyQt, has enabled you to understand a fairly complex application.

Understanding how the non-Qt part of the projects you'll encounter in the real world interacts with the Qt part of the code, will often be the main challenge you face as a Qt developer.

9.5. References

- https://en.wikipedia.org/wiki/GStreamer
- https://www.slideshare.net/DuncanMacleod4/detecting-gravitational-waves-in-python
- https://gstreamer.freedesktop.org/documentation/application-development/basics/elements.html#element-states
- https://gstreamer.freedesktop.org/documentation/application-development/basics/pads.html#dynamic-or-sometimes-pads
- https://doc.qt.io/qt-6/qmainwindow.html#setCentralWidget
- https://gstreamer.freedesktop.org/documentation/design/messages.html
- https://doc.qt.io/qt-6/qcombobox.html#activated
- https://doc.qt.io/qt-6/qabstractbutton.html
- https://github.com/kelvintan/qt5radio
- https://doc.qt.io/qt-6/qwidget.html
- https://doc.qt.io/qt-6/qwidget.html#winId
- https://doc.qt.io/qt-6/qplaintextedit.html
- https://brettviren.github.io/pygst-tutorial-org/pygst-tutorial.html

Appendix A. Multi-threading

Open the directory called "A" in the "Appendix" folder and run *thread-demo.py*.

Figure A.1. Threads demo

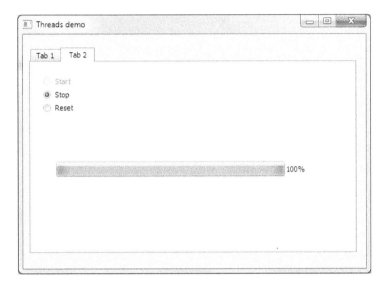

Ideally, you should be able to click start, have the progressbar slowly shift to 100% and it should stop when you click the "Stop" radio button. This doesn't happen though, try it for yourself and see. Once you click "Start" you have to wait for the progressbar to reach 100% before you can do anything else. You can't even switch tabs and the script appears to hang if you try to interact with it, as it ticks away to 100.

Why does this happen? Perhaps you've encountered something similar in your scripts or in other people's scripts. This occurs because execution flow is stuck inside the while loop shown in line 60 of *thread-demo.py*. By default, there is only one single thread running and everything else stops until the while loop completes.

To see the contrast, un-comment line 65 and run the script again. This time, you can stop the progressbar bar midway. And you can interact with other components for example, switching tabs as the progressbar ticks away. This time, the while loop is contained in a separate thread from the rest of the script logic.

What is a thread? A thread or a thread of execution is defined in computer science as the smallest unit that can be scheduled in an operating system. Threads are normally created by a fork of a computer script or program into two or more parallel (which is implemented on a single processor by multitasking) tasks. Threads are usually contained in processes. More than one thread can exist within the same process. These threads share the memory and the state of the process. In other words, they share the code or instructions and the values of its variables.

There are two different kinds of threads:

- Kernel threads
- User-space threads or user threads

Kernel threads are part of the operating system, while user-space threads are not implemented in the operating system kernel.

Every process has at least one thread, i.e., the process itself. A process can start multiple threads. The operating system executes these threads like parallel "processes". On a single processor machine, this parallelism is achieved by thread scheduling or time slicing. Looking back at our above example, instead of having to wait for the while-loop to finish, we can fork a parallel execution flow to deal with other user input processing.

However, it's important to note that threads only appear to be running in parallel. Python implements the Global Interpreter Lock(GIL), which prevents threads from running in parallel(even on multi-processor computers). Through task-switching, Python rapidly switches between many tasks and gives the illusion of parallel processing.

Threading can useful in applications that have a lot of downtime as they wait for user input or even network input.

A.1. How to implement threading

We've seen one way to implement this as shown in line 65, by using *Qapplication.processEvents()*. However, this is only a stopgap measure and should only be used occasionally when a program is performing a long operation. For Qt programming, we will use the *QThread* class for our multi-threading needs.

The generic structure of a threaded app is as follows:

```
1 from PyQt6 import QtCore
```

```
2
3 class YourThreadName(QtCore.QThread):
4
5     def __init__(self):
6         super(YourThreadName, self).__init__(parent)
7
8     def run(self):
9         # Thread code here
```

QThread is a simple class that you can pass arguments to when creating a new instance since it has a normal *__init__* method. Also, when you want to run the thread, you don't call the *run()* method itself, you call *start()* instead. Calling *run()* directly in some cases can freeze your main thread depending on how the run method is implemented in your thread.

In the code for *thread-demo-final.py* an argument is passed to the new instance. This argument contains the initial value for the progressbar. The thread is initialized and started as shown:

```
77 self.runThread = RunThread(parent=None,
counter_start=start_value)
78 self.runThread.start()
```

 Tip

In Qt we have an alternative to the callback technique: we use signals and slots. A signal is emitted when a particular event occurs. Qt's widgets have many predefined signals, but we can always subclass widgets to add our own signals to them. A slot is a function that is called in response to a particular signal. Qt's widgets have many pre-defined slots, but it is common practice to subclass widgets and add our own slots so that you can handle the signals that you are interested in.

```
76     def progressbar_counter(self, start_value=0):
77         self.runThread = RunThread(parent=None,
counter_start=start_value)
78         self.runThread.start() ▌1
```

```
79
    self.runThread.counter_value.connect(self.set_
    progressbar)
80
81        def set_progressbar(self, counter): 2
82            if not self.stopProgress:
83                self.progressBar.setValue(counter)
84
85 class RunThread(QtCore.QThread):
86
87        counter_value = QtCore.pyqtSignal(int) 3
88
89        def __init__(self, parent=None, counter_start
= 0):
90            super(RunThread, self).__init__(parent)
91            self.counter = counter_start
92            self.isRunning = True
93
94        def run(self):
95            while (self.counter < 100) and
(self.isRunning == True):
96                sleep(0.1) 4
97                self.counter += 1 5
98                print(self.counter) 6
99                self.counter_value.emit(self.counter) 7
100
101        def stop(self):
102            self.isRunning = False
103            print("Stopping Thread")
104            self.terminate()
```

1   This line initializes our thread and then calls its *run()* method on line 94.

4 5 After sleeping briefly, we update our counter value and print out a debug value.

6

7   This emits a signal. Its listener, that is, the slot that listens for the particular event was created on line 79.

2   This function is called every time our thread emits a signal. Basically what this does is increment by 1% the value of the progress bar. Approximately every tenth of a second, the progress bar value will increase slightly.

3   So far, we've only provided slots to connect to ready-made signals. This is how you create a signal and you *emit* its value as shown on line 99. Line 87 creates a signal that emits an integer argument.

A.2. References

- https://www.python-course.eu/threads.php
- https://en.wikipedia.org/wiki/Global_interpreter_lock
- https://doc.qt.io/qt-6/qcoreapplication.html#processEvents
- https://doc.qt.io/qt-6/signalsandslots.html
- https://doc.qt.io/qt-6/qthread.html

This page inten-
tionally left blank

Appendix B. Network Access Manager

In the chapter where we designed the Currency Exchange rates app, we used the *requests* module to communicate with a web service. It was intuitive and pretty easy to use. However, Qt also comes with its own network communication class called *QNetworkAccessManager*. Using it has one major advantage namely, it provides us with signals that we can use with other Qt widgets.

The Network Access API is constructed around one *QNetworkAccessManager* object, which holds the common configuration and settings for the requests it sends. It contains the proxy and cache configuration, as well as signals related to such issues and reply signals that can be used to monitor the progress of a network operation. One *QNetworkAccessManager* instance should be enough for the whole Qt application. Since *QNetworkAccessManager* is based on *QObject*, it can only be used from the thread it belongs to.

Once a *QNetworkAccessManager* object has been created, the application can use it to send requests over the network. A group of standard functions are supplied that take a request and optional data, and each return a *QNetworkReply* object. The returned object is used to obtain any data returned in response to the corresponding request.

The code below is found in *get.py*.

```
5 class MainWindow(QObject):
6     def __init__(self):
7         super().__init__()
8
9         target = "https://
www.riverbankcomputing.com/static/Docs/PyQt6/
index.html" ❶
10         request = QNetworkRequest(QUrl(target))
11
12         self.networkAccessManager =
QNetworkAccessManager() ❷
```

```
13          self.networkAccessManager.finished.
connect(self.onFinished) 3
14          self.networkAccessManager.get(request) 4
15
16      def onFinished(self, response): #response is an
object of type QNetworkReply
17          error = response.error() 5
18
19          if (error.NoError): 6
20              result = response.readAll() # you can
print this if you like
21              print("Response content type is:
"+response.header(QNetworkRequest.KnownHeaders.
ContentTypeHeader))
22              print("Server header is:
"+response.header(QNetworkRequest.KnownHeaders.
ServerHeader))
23              print("Server response time is:
"+response.header(QNetworkRequest.KnownHeaders.
LastModifiedHeader).toString())
24          else:
25              print("There was an error.
"+response.errorString())
26
27          self.windUp(response) 7
28
29      def windUp(self, replyObject): #replyObject is
an object of type QNetworkReply
30          #print("Network request completed!")
31          replyObject.deleteLater() 8
32          QCoreApplication.quit()
33
34
35 if __name__ == '__main__':
36
37      qApp = QCoreApplication(sys.argv) 9
```

```
38      w = MainWindow()
39      sys.exit(qApp.exec_())
```

1   The *QNetworkRequest* class holds a request to be sent with *QNetworkAccess-Manager*. *QNetworkRequest* is part of the Network Access API and is the class holding the information necessary to send a request over the network. It contains a URL and some ancillary information that can be used to modify the request.

2 3   We initialize our *QNetworkAccessManager* object. We pass it the *QNetworkRe-**4**   quest* object it will use and connect a slot which will be called after the request is completed.

5   We are inside the slot which means the network request is complete. Once the request is complete, Qt hands us back a response object of type *QNetworkReply*. We take our response and check it for errors.

6   This block executes if our network request completes successfully. We stored the resulting response in a variable called *result* and then we print out some server response headers.

Have a look at line 23 again. *response.header(QNetworkRequest.KnownHeaders.LastModifiedHeader)* returns an object of type *QDateTime*. To convert this into an easy to read format, we call the *toString()* method of *QDateTime*.

7   This line calls the *windUp()* method.

8   According to the PyQt documentation(https://doc.qt.io/qt-6/qnetworkaccess-manager.html#details), we must delete the *QNetworkReply* object after we finish with it. We do this by calling the *deleteLater()* method of our object.

9   Note that we're using *QCoreApplication* instead of *QApplication* like we've previously done. *QCoreApplication* is used to create PyQt applications that don't have a GUI. Just like GUI PyQt applications, they have one primary thread and may have any number of secondary threads.

B.1. References

- https://doc.qt.io/qt-6/qnetworkrequest.html#details
- https://doc.qt.io/qt-6/qnetworkrequest.html#KnownHeaders-enum
- https://doc.qt.io/qt-6/qnetworkreply.html

This page inten-
tionally left blank

Appendix C. Using Docker

This section will walk you through building a Docker image to run the scripts in this book. The author has tested all the troublesome scripts in this book and has found that they work fairly well in Docker. Please note that you will still need to set up *Qt Creator* and *pyuic* for yourself!

Windows users will need to set up Docker Desktop and Windows Subsystem for Linux(WSL2). They will need to install at least one Linux distro and enable Docker support in it. Instructions on how to do this can be found at:

https://docs.docker.com/desktop/wsl/

Linux users don't need Docker Desktop. Plain old Docker will be good enough. Whatever OS you use, please look up the appropriate documentation on the Docker website.

C.1. Initial setup

After setting everything up, start the daemon and run the following command to confirm that Docker is running:

```
docker info
```

If everything is properly set up and the daemon is running, information about your setup will be printed on your teminal.

C.1.1. Windows

The Dockerfile you need to build will be found in the Appendix C folder. Copy it to a folder and *cd* into that folder from the terminal. The command used to build the file is:

```
docker build -f Dockerfile.windows -t qttest .
```

After it finishes open a terminal(if you haven't already done so) in the Linux distro you installed. Please confirm that WSL integration for the distro chosen is enabled by going to **Settings>Resources>WSL Integration** from Docker Desktop.

 Tip

A full-size image of the following screenshot can be found in the *images* folder.

Figure C.1. WSL Integration

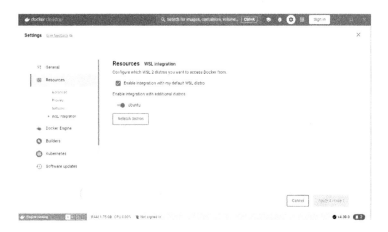

Drives in the Windows filesytem are represented as: */mnt/<drive name e.g. c>*.

Thus the path

```
C:\Users\PC\Desktop\pyqt6-2ndEd-master
```

will be represented as:

```
/mnt/c/Users/PC/Desktop/pyqt6-2ndEd-master
```

To run the second example in the folder for chapter 1, the following command was used:

```
docker run -it --rm -e DISPLAY=${DISPLAY} -v /tmp/.X11-
unix:/tmp/.X11-unix -v /mnt/c/Users/PC/Desktop/
pyqt6-2ndEd-master/:/home/pyqt6user/pyqt6book/ -e
 FILETORUN=1.*/simple1.py qttest
```

Figure C.2. simple1.py

The fourth example in the second chapter was run as follows:

```
docker run -it --rm -e DISPLAY=${DISPLAY} -v /tmp/.X11-
unix:/tmp/.X11-unix -v /mnt/c/Users/PC/Desktop/
pyqt6-2ndEd-master/:/home/pyqt6user/pyqt6book/ -e
 FILETORUN=2.*/position4.py qttest
```

Figure C.3. position4.py

The fifth example in the fourth chapter was run as follows:

```
docker run -it --rm -e DISPLAY=${DISPLAY} -v /tmp/.X11-
unix:/tmp/.X11-unix -v /mnt/c/Users/PC/Desktop/
pyqt6-2ndEd-master/:/home/pyqt6user/pyqt6book/ -e
 FILETORUN=4.*/widget5.py qttest
```

Figure C.4. widget5.py

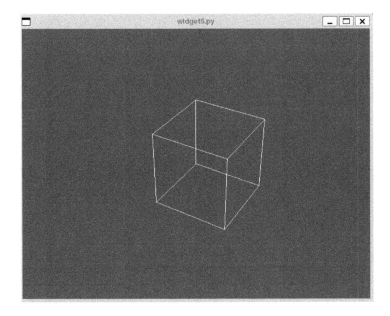

The last example in the eighth chapter was run as follows:

```
docker run -it --rm -e DISPLAY=${DISPLAY} -v /tmp/.X11-
unix:/tmp/.X11-unix -v /mnt/c/Users/PC/Desktop/
pyqt6-2ndEd-master/:/home/pyqt6user/pyqt6book/ -e
 FILETORUN=8.*/qt6radio.py -e PULSE_SERVER=/mnt/wslg/
PulseServer -v /mnt/wslg/:/mnt/wslg/ qttest
```

Figure C.5. qt6radio.py

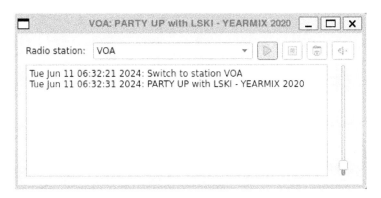

The ogg file player in chapter 8 was run using:

```
docker run -it --rm -e DISPLAY=${DISPLAY} -v /tmp/.X11-
unix:/tmp/.X11-unix -v /mnt/c/Users/PC/Desktop/
pyqt6-2ndEd-master/:/home/pyqt6user/pyqt6book/ -e
 FILETORUN=8.*/baby.py -e PULSE_SERVER=/mnt/wslg/
PulseServer -v /mnt/wslg/:/mnt/wslg/ qttest
```

C.1.2. Other operating systems

The Dockerfile you need to build will be found in the Appendix C folder. Copy it to a folder and *cd* into that folder from the terminal. The command used to build the file is:

```
docker build -f Dockerfile -t qttest .
```

Similar commands can be used on *nix systems. The following are some of the commands executed on Linux:

```
docker run -it --rm -e DISPLAY=$DISPLAY -v /tmp/.X11-
unix:/tmp/.X11-unix -v /home/pc/work/pyqt6-2ndEd-
master/:/home/pyqt6user/pyqt6book/ -e FILETORUN=1.*/
simple1.py qttest
```

```
docker run -it --rm -e DISPLAY=$DISPLAY -v /tmp/.X11-
unix:/tmp/.X11-unix -v /home/pc/work/pyqt6-2ndEd-
master/:/home/pyqt6user/pyqt6book/ -e FILETORUN=2.*/
position4.py qttest
```

```
docker run -it --rm -e DISPLAY=$DISPLAY -v /tmp/.X11-
unix:/tmp/.X11-unix -v /home/pc/work/pyqt6-2ndEd-
master/:/home/pyqt6user/pyqt6book/ -e FILETORUN=4.*/
widget5.py qttest
```

```
docker run -it --rm -e DISPLAY=$DISPLAY -v /tmp/.X11-
unix:/tmp/.X11-unix -v /home/pc/work/pyqt6-2ndEd-
master/:/home/pyqt6user/pyqt6book/ -e FILETORUN=8.*/
hello.py qttest
```

```
docker run -it -e DISPLAY=$DISPLAY --privileged=true --
device=/dev/snd:/dev/snd -v /tmp/.X11-unix:/tmp/.X11-
unix -v /home/pc/work/pyqt6-2ndEd-master/:/home/
pyqt6user/pyqt6book/ -e FILETORUN=8.*/baby.py qttest
```

```
docker run -it -e DISPLAY=$DISPLAY --privileged=true --
device=/dev/snd:/dev/snd -v /tmp/.X11-unix:/tmp/.X11-
unix -v /home/pc/work/pyqt6-2ndEd-master/:/home/
pyqt6user/pyqt6book/ -e FILETORUN=8.*/qt6radio.py qttest
```

This page inten-
tionally left blank

Appendix D. Python's _name_ variable

This is a follow-up of the explanation provided in Chapter 1.

When you get the OS to run a script for you for example by typing:

python3 simple.py

the interpreter automatically sets a few special variables like _name_ and then executes the code in the file.

The code below is found in *test.py* of the Appendix, D folder.

```python
 1 print("before import")
 2 import math
 3
 4 print("before functionA")
 5 def functionA():
 6     print("Function A")
 7
 8 print("before functionB")
 9 def functionB():
10     print("Function B {}".format(math.sqrt(100)))
11
12 print("before __name__ guard")
13 if __name__ == '__main__':
14     functionA()
15     functionB()
16 print("after __name__ guard")
```

When you run it from the command line, you get the following output:

```
before import
before functionA
before functionB
```

```
before __name__ guard
Function A
Function B 10.0
after __name__ guard
```

When the script is "passed" directly to the interpreter, the __name__ variable is given the value __main__. The script then sequentially executes. The if conditional on line 13 is found to be true and functions A and B are run.

The code below is found in *display.py* in the same folder.

```
import test

print("before __name__ guard of display.py")
if __name__ == '__main__':
    print("Konichiwa!")
print("after __name__ guard of display.py")
```

When you run it from the command line, you get the following output:

```
before import
before functionA
before functionB
before __name__ guard
after __name__ guard
before __name__ guard of display.py
Konichiwa!
after __name__ guard of display.py
```

It imports the module *test.py* and sequentially executes it. However, this time the test in line 13 of *test.py* fails, and the two functions in it aren't run.

www.ingramcontent.com/pod-product-compliance
Lightning Source LLC
LaVergne TN
LVHW081345050326
832903LV00024B/1320